BIBLE-CARRYING CHRISTIANS

BIBLE-CARRYING
CHRISTIANS

CONSERVATIVE PROTESTANTS AND SOCIAL POWER

DAVID HARRINGTON WATT

OXFORD
UNIVERSITY PRESS

2002

OXFORD
UNIVERSITY PRESS

Oxford   New York

Athens   Auckland   Bangkok   Bogotá   Buenos Aires   Cape Town
Chennai   Dar es Salaam   Delhi   Florence   Hong Kong   Istanbul   Karachi
Kolkata   Kuala Lumpur   Madrid   Melbourne   Mexico City   Mumbai   Nairobi
Paris   São Paulo   Shanghai   Singapore   Taipei   Tokyo   Toronto   Warsaw

and associated companies in
Berlin   Ibadan

Copyright © 2002 by David Harrington Watt

Published by Oxford University Press, Inc.,
198 Madison Avenue, New York, New York 10016

Oxford is a registered trademark of Oxford University Press

Library of Congress Cataloging-in-Publication Data
Watt, David Harrington.
Bible-carrying Christians : conservative Protestants and social power /
David Harrington Watt.
   p.   cm.
Includes bibliographical references and index.
ISBN 0-19-506834-3
1. Christianity and politics—Pennsylvania—Philadelphia—Case studies.
2. Protestant churches—Pennsylvania—Philadelphia—Case studies.
3. Conservatism—Religious aspects—Christianity—Case studies.   I. Title.
BR560.P5 W38 2002
306 .6'804'0973—dc21   2001021587

9 8 7 6 5 4 3 2 1

Printed in the United States of America
on acid-free paper

TO LAURA

Slaves, obey your earthly masters with fear and trembling, in singleness of heart as you obey Christ.

EPHESIANS 6.5, NRSV

The LORD is a haven for the oppressed, a haven in times of trouble.

PSALMS 9.10, NRSV

When words are strange or disturbing to you, try to sense where they come from and what has nourished the lives of others. . . . Think it possible that you may be mistaken.

QUAKER FAITH AND PRACTICE, I.02

Believers and disbelievers assert there is no middle ground: You are either one or the other. You cannot both believe and disbelieve. But that is precisely what it means to be under conviction. You do not believe in the sense of public declarations, but you gradually come to respond to, and interpret, and act in the world as if you were a believer. It is a state of unconscious belief, experienced with more or less turmoil and anxiety, depending on how strong your disbelieving voices are. It also depends for the ethnographer on how adamant your colleagues are about the "dangers" of doing "this kind of fieldwork." I was given to think my credibility depended on my resisting any experience of born-again belief. The irony is that this space between belief and disbelief, or rather the paradoxical space of overlap, is also the space of ethnography. We must enter it to do our work.

HARDING, "CONVICTED BY THE HOLY SPIRIT," 178

ACKNOWLEDGMENTS

I AM GRATEFUL to three research assistants—Anthony Broyles, Pam Hayden, and Sally Dwyer-McNulty—for the hours they spent on this book. The book is based on fieldwork, conducted between October 1991 and December 1993 in three churches: the Oak Grove Church, the Philadelphia Mennonite Fellowship, and the Philadelphia Church of Christ.[1] The book could not have been written were it not for the many kindnesses extended to me by the members of these three congregations. I am especially grateful to the six women—identified in the text as Jane Thomas, Susan Bateson, Emma Roberts, Sarah Mather, Margaret Drake, and Eleanor Gregory—who allowed themselves to be interviewed by Hayden and Dwyer-McNulty[2] and whose answers helped me to see things that I would otherwise have missed about the way in which social power flows through Christian congregations.

Bruce Comens, who teaches English at Temple University, was kind enough to visit all three churches, and his essays on what he saw there were of enormous help to me. Don Browning and Robert Wuthnow provided invaluable assistance in designing the questionnaires that guided the interviews with the six congregants.

Portions of this book were also read at various times by Browning, Wuthnow, Margaret Bendroth, Courtney Bender, Pamela Couture, Allen F. Davis, R. Marie Griffith, D. G. Hart, James Hudnut-Beumler, William R. Hutchison, Janet Jakobsen, Lee Junker, Louise Kidder, Robert Kidder, Laura Levitt, Colleen McDannell, Martin Marty, Bonnie Miller-McLemore, Esther Mürer, Robert Orsi, Anthony Prete, Edward Queen II, Daniel Sack, Barbara Savage, Leigh Schmidt, Herbert Simons, Thomas Tweed, Heidi Rolland Unruh, Judith Weisenfeld, and Diane Winston. I am more grateful than I can say for the help these friendly critics have given me.

The entire book was reviewed with great care by Alison Anderson and Maud Lavin; their suggestions on how to improve the manuscript were extraordinarily helpful. The book was also strengthened by the support of Kathryn Damiano, John Harding, Peter Haynes, Janet Stokes, and Raymond Dewey Watt, Jr.

The research on which the book is based was supported by a series of generous grants from the Lilly Endowment. It was supported, too, by grants from the Religion, Family and Culture Project of the University of Chicago and from the Research and Study Leave Committee of the College of Arts and Sciences of Temple University.

CONTENTS

BIBLE-CARRYING CHRISTIANS

ONE

FIELDWORK

CHRISTIAN CONGREGATIONS

For nearly two millennia, followers of Christ have been forming themselves into congregations, which have performed a wide variety of functions. They have distributed food to people who are hungry, cared for the sick, and buried the dead. They have provided excitement to people who were bored and tranquility to people who were in turmoil. They have created buildings in which God's praises could be sung and in which God could be asked to pour out blessings upon the human race.

The congregations created by Christians have also, of course, devoted a good deal of attention to catechism. In Christian congregations, people have learned stories about God's chosen people and about the relationships between them and their God. They have learned formulas that purport to give hints about what God is like. They have learned how to sing. They have learned how to pray.

They have also learned a great deal about which sort of human power relationships are "natural" and which are not. Is it natural for people who do not know Latin to defer to those who do? For emperors to defer to bishops? For slaves to defer to the free? For people who are sexually active to defer to those who are celibate? For the ignorant to defer to the learned? For the uncivilized to defer to the civilized? For people who are rich to defer to people who have taken vows of poverty? For the young to defer to the middle-aged? For the middle-aged to defer to the ancient? For people who are not Jewish and who do not follow the Torah to defer to those who are and do?

The process of teaching people the answers to such questions is, of course, an ancient one. Traces of it can be found in the Christian Scriptures and in the writings of the church fathers. They can be found, too, in the primary sources that tell us what we know about the history of the church in the Middle Ages and in the modern world. And, of course, teaching Christians which sorts of power relations are normal and acceptable and which are not is something that congregations still do. In fact, it is not at all clear that Christian congregations could cease to offer such instruction without thereby ceasing to be Christian congregations.

It is certain, in any case, that each of the three Philadelphia congregations that this book describes devoted a huge amount of energy to teaching its members which sorts of social relations are normal. The first congregation, Oak Grove Church, was located in a section of Philadelphia that was once solidly working class but had in recent years fallen on hard times. The congregation operated a Christian school designed to insulate children from the influence of "secular humanism." It also provided support for a number of political activities aimed at limiting the power that "secular humanists" exercise over the U.S. government. The second church, the Philadelphia Mennonite Fellowship, met in a rented building a few blocks from the University of Pennsylvania. A number of its members attempted to resist attitudes and behaviors that they saw as "corporate" or "warlike" and therefore un-Christian. The third church, the Philadelphia Church of Christ, placed a great deal of emphasis on trying to attract new members. The leaders of this church described it, with a modicum of plausibility, as one of the fastest growing Protestant congregations in the city.

All three churches differed in one important respect from the congregations I am used to attending, where those who were in the habit of carrying their own copy of the Bible to church on Sunday morning would have been thought odd. We just don't do that. The people at those three did do that.

In the course of my fieldwork I gradually came to think of the people who attended the three churches as Bible-carrying Christians. That category came to seem less problematic than the categories I started with: conservative Protestant and evangelical. It turned out that only a minority of these people were willing to describe themselves as evangelicals or as conservative Protestants. And the category Bible-carrying also has the advantage of emphasizing the degree to which all three churches saw the Bible as an indispensable and utterly trustworthy guide to the nature of the universe in which we live. At all three churches, questions—no matter what topic they concerned—tended to produce answers that circled back to the same formula: "Well, the Bible says. . . ."

So, then, this book is meant to be an ethnographic analysis of the churches in which Bible-carrying Christians assemble. There are hundreds of thousands of such churches in the United States, and it is now generally acknowledged that they play a crucial role in shaping contemporary American culture and politics. If America were not permeated by such institutions, if such institutions were somehow to be replaced by a set of pagan worship groups or by an alliance of Buddhist meditation centers or even by a string of liberal Episcopal congregations whose rectors had all been deeply influenced by the work of Paul Tillich and H. Richard Niebuhr, America as a whole would become a very different place—not better, necessarily, but undeniably different.

And if such a transformation were to occur, the sort of power relations that seem natural might very well shift rather dramatically. In the contemporary United States, Bible-carrying churches offer instruction to millions of people about which sort of power relationships are normal and which are suspect. If that were not the case, Americans' assumptions about those matters could well be very different. Thus, at a very basic level, Americans' political assumptions are decisively shaped by Bible-carrying Christian churches.

It seems odd, therefore, that students of American culture and politics have produced so few careful descriptions of the way in which Bible-carrying Christian churches shape our understanding of which power relations are suspect and which are not. My dissatisfaction with the paucity of such descriptions is what led me to write this book, where I explore which forms of social power are, and are not, naturalized in Bible-carrying Christian churches. (In this context, to "naturalize" is to treat something that is actually historically constructed as though it were self-evidently "natural" and therefore beyond questioning.) As I investigate that topic, I pay special attention to the ways in which these churches do and do not naturalize the authority of the U.S. state, of modern corporations, of ministers, of men, and of heterosexuals.

A METHOD

While I was doing the research for this book, an acquaintance asked: "Are the people in these churches going to give you new information?" I replied that I would be reluctant to say that they were. To me, saying that they were going to "give" me "information" rang false. Ethnographic work is not a matter of going into the field in search of "data" that "informants" "possess." Data are not things that one person can give to another.

My ethnographic work, as I understood it, was largely a way of giving myself a set of experiences that I hoped would make it possible for me to see things about the world that I could not see if I had not had them. It was an attempt to make myself a little less parochial.[1]

It was also an attempt to see whether ethnography might help get at some matters that tend to elude historians. Students of the history of religion in the United States are always tempted to define our fields with terms that we take from women and (more often) men with enough power to get their ideas into print and then into libraries and archives, where they can be conveniently consulted.[2] Sometimes historians of religion in the United States have resisted that temptation. More often we have yielded. Turning to ethnography might enable us to see things that we could not see by reading formal texts.

AN ETHNOGRAPHER

The first time I attended services at Oak Grove, a man started talking to me almost immediately, introducing himself as Ed. After I said hello and gave him my name, Ed said something similar to "I discern that you are born again." I said that I was a practicing Christian. He aked if I had been born again. I said I was raised a Baptist, that I had believed I had been converted when I was 6 years old, and that I had been baptized. Ed said something such as "You think! Don't you *know*?" He then tried to win me to Christ on the spot. This was, I gathered, going to be a four-step process that would end with a prayer like the one in *Four Spiritual Laws* (a famous, widely circulating evangelical pamphlet written by Bill Bright of Campus Crusade for Christ).[3] The first step involved reading a verse in Romans 3. I read the verse—which I actually agreed with—but then put an end to the process: "I feel as if you are trying to manipulate me." Ed said that nothing could be further from the truth. He was just trying to keep me from spending eternity in hell.

I found it impossible to do my fieldwork in a way that made Ed—and most of the other people at Oak Grove and the two other churches—conclude that I was observing what was going on from a "neutral" perspective. They did not believe that such a perspective existed, and their suspicions were no doubt well founded.

In any case, it would be foolish to pretend that this book presents an unfiltered reflection of the congregations in which I worked. It is rather a set of reflections on some of the things I saw and heard while I was working there. Of course, what I saw and heard was determined by the set of questions I took with me into the field, as well as by the experiences I had there. When I heard something that connected in my mind with those questions, I became alert.

I became alert, too, when I heard something that seemed either particularly close to or particularly far away from the sorts of experiences that I have had at other times in my life. For that reason, I want to say a few words about the other—that is, the nonethnographic—experiences I have had. As I do so, I will be drawing on some autobiographical notes I made just after my first venture into the field. These experiences are not terribly dramatic. They did, however, strongly affect what I noticed and failed to notice while I was in the field.

Before I began, I read a number of essays and books about fieldwork, some of which suggested writing a brief autobiographical essay before one went into the field. I wrote my notes, however, the week after I started, and the following is a revised version.

Throughout the fieldwork on which this book is based, I was dating an artist named Miriam. Miriam, who worked for the Episcopal Church, was in her late 30s and had a daughter named Elizabeth.

Adjectives I have heard applied to me include *tall, shy, friendly, introspective, funny, intense, spacey, distant, repressed, hard to get to know, athletic,* and *awkward.* Most people do tend to like me and to find that at a certain point I become "hard to get to know." I look, I think, like a college professor. But I almost never wear a jacket and tie, and during the years in which I was doing my fieldwork people sometimes took me for a graduate student.

My mother is a schoolteacher, raised in rural Alabama. Her parents farmed land they did not own and worked in cotton mills. She was raised a Southern Baptist and attended a Baptist college and a Baptist seminary.

My father works part time now as a schoolteacher, as well as a Southern Baptist minister. For most of his adult life he has made his living in church work, and certainly "pastor" is a more important part of his identity than "teacher." He was raised in the suburbs of Washington, D.C., in a middle-class family. His father had a college degree, and his stepmother (the women I called Grandmother) had a doctorate.

My sister is eleven years younger than I am and more athletic; she has always been better at baseball, volleyball, and basketball, although we do have this in common: we both turn beet red in the course of a hard-fought basketball game. My sister is arguably less religious than I am: churches have let her down more than once. On the other hand, she is still a member in good standing of a Southern Baptist church. She has three children—a daughter (born in 1989) and two sons (born in 1992 and 1998)—who regularly attend Sunday School.

My parents moved to Louisville, Kentucky, in 1955 or 1956, and I was born there in 1957. I don't remember anything about Kentucky. I do remember Alabama, which is where our family lived (mostly) between 1959 and 1966. Indeed, I believe I remember hearing men I knew well saying that they would kill Martin Luther King, Jr., if he tried to come to our church.

Our family moved to the deserts of California in 1966. I stayed there through my first year of college (I went to a junior college my freshman year). In 1976, I moved to Berkeley to attend the University of California. I lived in a co-op; worked as a janitor; and studied history, which I loved. In 1980 I moved to Boston to study the history or religion in the United States. There is a sense in which I reinvented my self-presentation at Berkeley. I then modified it—made it slightly more refined—in Boston. But not all of Boston's effects were quite that predictable. I was a liberal when I left Berkeley; when I left Boston I had somehow moved further to the left.

Even before I went to Berkeley (probably sometime around 1973) I stopped going to Southern Baptist churches and started attending less conservative ones. It was not a move that made either of my parents particularly happy, but it actually created less ill will than any of us would have predicted. I am still a nonfundamentalistic Protestant and still fairly devout. On most weekdays, I find some time to pray or meditate. On most Sundays, I make my way to a service at a Protestant congregation in downtown Philadelphia.

TWO

PHILADELPHIA

RELIGION

During my fieldwork, I often had occasion to look at Philadelphia's skyline, which seldom struck me as overtly religious. It was defined by modern and postmodern buildings that were devoted to manufacturing or commerce rather than to worship.[1]

But Philadelphia's early history was, of course, closely intertwined with religion, and traces of religion's historic importance and its continuing presence were not hard to find as I walked or drove around the city. William Penn, the Quaker who founded the city, still stood atop City Hall. Rodeph Shalom, the first Ashkenazic congregation to be organized in the Americas, still met two-thirds of a mile north of City Hall. The Liberty Bell, which was located about two-thirds of a mile east of City Hall, still carried an inscription (which was a little hard to make out) from Leviticus: "proclaim liberty throughout all the land unto all the inhabitants thereof."[2] Mother Bethel African Methodist Episcopal Church, the congregation out of which grew one of the largest denominations in the United States, stood a few blocks south of the bell. Church steeples were scattered through nearly all the neighborhoods in the city. A number of neighborhoods had mosques, and a few had Buddhist temples.

At the time of my fieldwork, Philadelphia's newspapers did not devote much space to religion. I cannot remember any day when the number of column inches of religious news was not dwarfed by the number of inches reporting on such subjects as the performance of the financial markets, the activities of professional and quasi-professional sports teams, and products manufactured by the entertainment industry. But religion did, of course, get some press coverage, and what coverage it did get often resulted in the sort of story that caught my eye. So, by the time I had completed my fieldwork, my scrapbooks contained hundreds of newspaper clippings about religion, many of which focused on the relationship between religion and politics. They convinced me that religious groups did *sometimes* influence the outcome of political struggles that had a direct affect on the lives of Philadelphians.

They include, for instance, stories about an attempt to get Philadelphia's City Council to grant legal protections to gay and lesbian couples, a political drive that was vociferously opposed by religious leaders. Cardinal Anthony J. Bevilacqua, the Black Clergy of Philadelphia, and the Majlis As-Shura Council of Mosques all let it be known that they thought that granting such protections would be a terrible mistake.

The clippings also include a number of stories about abortion and religion. When I started to compile my scrapbook, it was not terribly difficult for women in Philadelphia to obtain legal abortions. But by the time I had finished, the Commonwealth of Pennsylvania had adopted legislation that made it more difficult for women living anywhere within its borders to have access to legal abortions. Several of the stories that I clipped suggested that this legislation would not have been adopted without the efforts of some religious institutions and some religious people.

The tendency of religious organizations to become embroiled in political controversies was one of the reasons—though perhaps not the most important one—that these organizations were often portrayed unfavorably in the newspapers. Some of the stories focused on what might be seen as the religious groups' attempts to impose their particular moral standards on the broader society. Others depicted religious groups as dangerous cults that preyed on the credulous or were seedbeds for terrorism.[3]

Religious people were often portrayed as proponents of censorship. They were accused of practicing their religion in places—like buildings owned by the school district—where it was inappropriate for them to do so. They were linked to antisemitism, to discrimination against homosexuals and women, and to the murders of doctors who had performed abortions. So, if all you knew about religion was what you learned from reading my scrapbooks, you might have concluded that it is indeed an infamous thing and ought to be crushed. You might also have concluded that most of the city's religious groups had, as a newspaper article noted in April 1993, almost completely "abandoned the poor." Such evaluations, common in the early 1990s, contained a good deal of truth.

Almost all the religious institutions in the Philadelphia region were subjected to tremendous financial pressures in the early 1990s. Many responded to these pressures by concentrating more of their resources in the suburbs and in relatively prosperous parts of the city than in poor neighborhoods. The Roman Catholic Archdiocese of Philadelphia, for example, in deciding which parishes and schools to keep open and which to close, seemed to be moving itself away from the poor and toward people with money. Those actions, which were widely reported in the press, angered many Catholics. Indeed, some Catholics were so angry that they took part in an exorcism of the archdiocese's headquarters. The ritual was an attempt, they said, to rid the building of the demons of greed that had possessed it.

You could find little in my scrapbooks to indicate that the exorcism had had any effect. They do suggest, however, that it would be wrong to say either that religious organizations in Philadelphia had completely abandoned the poor or that the poor in Philadelphia had completely abandoned religious organizations. Some poor people who lived in Philadelphia participated regularly in worship services. There is good reason to suppose that some of them organized their lives around these services and what these services represented.

Some of Philadelphia's religious groups sponsored programs that seemed to be of some help to poor people who were addicted to drugs or alcohol, who were having difficulty in raising their children as well as they wished to, who were HIV positive, or who were having trouble getting enough to eat. My scrapbooks do not indicate that these programs worked perfectly or even particularly well. Certainly they did not work well enough to make Philadelphia a good city in which to be poor. But they did perhaps make Philadelphia a somewhat less awful place in which to be poor than it would have been otherwise.

Sometimes persons associated with religious groups—I am thinking particularly of a Roman Catholic sister named Mary Scullion—drew on anachronistic sacred texts to say interesting things about Philadelphia. Scullion said, for instance, that the homelessness in Philadelphia and the lousy schools in the city were caused by idol worship—worship like that denounced in the prophetic books of the Hebrew Bible—including the idol of money. She said that until that sort of worship was replaced or supplemented by other sorts, the schools would stay bad and women and men would continue to sleep on the streets.

From time to time, religious groups in Philadelphia tried to act against, rather than simply comment on, activities that they thought had deleterious effects on the city and were motivated by the love of money. For example, in July 1993 a group of people led by the president of the Black Clergy of Philadelphia and Vicinity marched on the streets in North Philadelphia (the part of town in which Temple University is located), painting over billboards that encouraged the purchase of alcohol and tobacco. The protestors called this defacement "blackwashing."

Religious groups, however, did not engage in such direct actions against corporate-sponsored propaganda very often. And when they did so, they certainly could not count on representatives of the government to ensure their right, as they saw it, to the free exercise of their religion. The leader of the blackwashing protest—as anyone who knew the history of church-state relations in the United States might well have predicted—was arrested.

Although the congregations that I visited between 1991 and 1993 did not get much attention in Philadelphia's newspapers, the Philadelphia Church of Christ was the subject of a story, broadcast on one of the local news programs, that portrayed the group (I was told) as a dangerous cult. Also, I do remember seeing a very short story in the *Inquirer*, reporting that the church was sponsoring a cleanup day to help the residents of one of the poorest neighborhoods get rid of some of the debris there. I cannot recall seeing any other references to the church in any of the Philadelphia papers.

A picture of one of the members of the Philadelphia Mennonite Fellowship appeared in the *Inquirer* on August 10, 1992. She was taking part in a meeting that commemorated the forty-seventh anniversary of the bombing of Nagasaki and which drew attention to the links between the University of Pennsylvania and the Pentagon. And there were a number of stories in both the *Inquirer* and the *Daily News* about a meeting in Philadelphia in the summer of 1993 that was attended by many members of the Mennonite Fellowship. That meeting, which attracted Mennonites from throughout the United States, was the first to be held in the city's controversial new convention center; it included some people who went out of their way to scold the city for devoting so much of its energy to building impressive new buildings and so little to meeting the needs of its poorer residents. But I do not recall that the Mennonite Fellowship was mentioned by name in any of the papers I was reading while I was doing my fieldwork, nor was there even a single reference to the members of Oak Grove Church, to the school that was affiliated with the church, or to the church itself.

SEGREGATION

When I came to Philadelphia in the spring of 1986 for a job interview at Temple University, I spent part of my time at Temple's campus in North Philadelphia and part in Center City, where my hotel was located. Most of the people in Center City were white and appeared to be prosperous. North Philadelphia included some of the poorest neighborhoods I had ever seen, and most of these residents were black.[4] Ever since that first visit, I have tended to think of Philadelphia as a city in which class divisions, long linked to racial and ethnic divisions, shape every aspect of the lives of its people. That tendency is no doubt partly a result of my own proclivities. I have long had a strong interest in class analysis.

And—it is important to be clear about this—not everyone who lived in Philadelphia during those years was either very rich or very poor, and not one of the congregations discussed in this book was made up of people who were very rich or extremely poor. They were, however, people who stood some chance of becoming very poor, and they were people whose neighbors bought lottery tickets in hopes of becoming very rich.

So, my tendency to focus on wealth and poverty when I thought about the city was, I argue, a plausible interpretation of the social circumstances in which the people whose churches I was visiting found themselves. It was also—and though this is obvious it is worth noting explicitly—a plausible interpretation of the circumstances in which I found myself.

At that time, I lived on the border between Center City and South Philadelphia. When I left my apartment, walked east two and a half blocks, turned left (north), and walked four blocks, I would find myself in the middle of a park called Rittenhouse Square. Although the park was owned by the city of Philadelphia, it was very well maintained, largely by private funds. The statues in the park were burnished; the fountain never overflowed; and the flowers, grass, and trees were all carefully tended. On most days the park was free—or at least, almost free—from trash. Clothing stores, condos, hotels, apartment buildings, bars, restaurants, bookstores, art galleries, and theaters surrounded the park. Many, but not all, were well beyond my budget. When the weather was nice, businesspeople—and lots of other people who were well dressed—sat on the benches in the park. They acted as though the park belonged to them—or rather, I suppose, to us—and as though the beggars with whom it had to be shared were, at best, nuisances to be minimized.[5]

When I left my apartment, walked east two and a half blocks, turned right (south), and walked four blocks, I would find myself at the corner of Nineteenth and Christian Streets. This neighborhood had a good deal in common with the neighborhoods just south of Oak Grove Church and also with those just north of Philadelphia Mennonite Fellowship.

The white people in this neighborhood could have been labeled urban pioneers or people who had some business at the post office on the corner. Most of the people who lived near Nineteenth and Christian were black. When they spoke, I could sometimes hear a touch of the accents of the upper South. City services were not absent from the neighborhood: public buses were on the streets, public schools were nearby, and there was gas service from a city-owned works. Police cars patrolled the area, and officers would respond when residents called 911. Trash was picked up by the city every week.

The city did not even pretend, however, to offer the same level of services to the people who lived here as it did to those who lived or worked in what was known as the Center City District. South of South Street, the streets and sidewalks were in bad repair and were dirtier than the sidewalks and streets further north.[6] Many of the row houses in the neighborhood were tended carefully. None of them, however, was ostentatious. Some had not received much attention in recent years, and some were abandoned.[7]

There were not many businesses near Nineteenth and Christian. There was a pharmacy, restaurants, delicatessens, and bars, none of them beyond my budget. Even when I dressed down, I showed that I had more money than most of the people who lived in this neighborhood. South of South Street, one rarely saw people who were dressed fashionably.

Some people were dressed well, but others were dressed as though they did not have steady incomes.[8]

There were lots of churches—mostly Protestant. Their services were rarely overcrowded; in fact, the congregations were sometimes fairly small. The churches did, however, continue to hold regular services. On Sunday mornings it always seemed at though one could not walk for more than a couple of minutes without seeing someone who was on the way to or from church. It was hard to imagine that the images of God that were embedded in the rituals within the walls of these churches had much in common with those in the churches near Rittenhouse Square: different lives; different gods.

POLITICAL ECONOMY

The people who lived in Philadelphia in the early 1990s tended to align themselves, though not in a particularly passionate way, with the Democratic party. In 1992, there were about 727,000 registered Democrats and only about 213,000 registered Republicans. Philadelphians tended to vote Democratic, too. In the 1991 mayoral election Ed Rendell, the Democratic candidate, received over twice as many votes as the Republican candidate, Joseph Egan. In the 1992 presidential election, about 132,000 Philadelphians voted for George Bush; about 430,000 voted for Bill Clinton.

Philadelphia was a city with a good deal of ethnic and racial heterogeneity. According to a survey conducted by the U.S. Bureau of the Census, in 1990 about 89,000 Hispanics, 43,000 Asians and Pacific Islanders, 848,000 whites, and 631,000 blacks were living in the city. In the early 1990s, Philadelphia was highly segregated. Indeed, by some measures, it was one of the most segregated cities in the nation,[9] To be sure, Philadelphia did have some racially integrated neighborhoods.[10] However, 62 percent of the African Americans who lived in Philadelphia lived in census tracts that were at least 90 percent black, and 64 percent of the white Philadelphians lived in census tracts that were at least 90 percent white.[11]

Lines between blacks and whites were, more often than not, reinforced by lines between economic classes. In the city's predominantly black neighborhoods, more than 35 percent of all residents lived below the poverty line. For the city as a whole, the figure was about 20 percent. In predominantly black neighborhoods, the median annual household income was about $15,000; the comparable figure for the city as a whole was about $25,000.

By the international standards that prevailed in the early 1990s, a median annual income of $25,000 was, of course, high rather than low. And no one could have denied that some people in Philadelphia were paid very well. A *Forbes* survey determined that in 1992 the median total compensation for chief executive officers (CEOs) in Philadelphia was $1.75 million. In that year, there were only three cities in the United States where CEOs were paid a higher average salary.[12] The city had, however, been losing jobs for decades.[13] In 1960 there were 1 million jobs in Philadelphia; in 1993 there were 760,000. Many of the lost jobs were in the manufacturing sector of the city's economy. In 1960 there were 300,000 such jobs; in 1993 there were 72,000.

The lack of jobs, especially of jobs that paid well, was a part of the quotidian reality of Philadelphians. The fears it created were sometimes visible, unless I was mistaken, on my neighbors' faces. And those fears were also evident, as I discovered during the course of my fieldwork, in the prayer meetings and Bible studies conducted at Protestant churches.[14]

The fears also played a role in shaping the political culture. As seen by the political and government leaders of Philadelphia, the city was competing with other places in the state, the nation, and the world. This competition revolved around the creation of a favorable climate in which to do business. Cities that established a favorable business climate would reap the rewards: jobs for their inhabitants and a strong tax base.

The newspapers portrayed Philadelphia as failing to create such a climate, a failure seen to be at the heart of its present difficulties. So in the early 1990s, the political and government leaders were eager to prove to the business community that they were going to do whatever it took to make the city the sort of place in which the business community could fulfill all its needs. When companies threatened to leave, aides to the mayor would do all they could to make sure that they did not. When companies raised the possibility of relocating within the city—a rather rare occurrence—political and government leaders treated representatives of those companies as though they were princes. The city's political and government leaders never actually took out an advertisement in the *Wall Street Journal* that said: "We are desperate for jobs. We desperately need to shore up our tax base. We will do anything your company asks of us to get you to come here." But they might as well have.[15]

In the last few decades, some of the people who worked for Philadelphia's city government or who held one its many public offices have been convicted of extortion and other crimes. More than one of those persons were treated as returning heroes after serving their time in prison, partly because Philadelphians did not believe that it made a lot of sense to differentiate too sharply between those who were "corrupt" and those who were engaging in politics as usual. The people knew that some of the ways in which politicians and government officials chased after money were, technically speaking, illegal, and they knew that others were not. They also knew that money-gathering activities were a crucial part of local politics and local government and that if all the city's politicians and government officials stopped chasing after money, politics and government—as those of us who live in Philadelphia have come to know them—would cease to exist.[16]

Philadelphia's cultural institutions, like its political ones, were largely steered by money.[17] During my fieldwork, Philadelphia's institutions did not rival those of New York, nor were they quite equal to those in Boston, Chicago, Los Angeles, San Francisco, or Washington, D.C. But they were still, by most standards, impressive. The ballet and the opera company were very good; the art museum and the orchestra were both first-rate. Philadelphia had one great research university, the University of Pennsylvania, within its city limits, and several other good colleges and universities—LaSalle, Drexel, Loyola, St. Joseph's, and Temple—were scattered throughout the city. Moreover, several highly regarded institutions—Swarthmore, Haverford, and Bryn Mawr—were located in the suburbs.

All these cultural and educational institutions were under tremendous economic pressures in the early 1990s. Many of them were making determined efforts to bring themselves to the attention of people who could provide them with the money they needed. One of the effects of those efforts was a relative lack of attention to the needs of people without much money. Whenever my fieldwork took me to one of the poorer neighborhoods, Philadelphia's famous educational and cultural institutions always seemed a long way away.

The financial efforts included a set of marketing campaigns, in which people with money were sometimes described as "potential customers" to whom educational and cultural institutions needed to make more "sales." Art and education were often constructed, at institutions that ran such campaigns, as products to be consumed by wealthy customers. People who worked at these institutions were told they had to keep their productivity high. Boards of trustees behaved as if their institutions had to be steered, in the final analysis, by the logic of the market.

Thus, when Temple University found itself going through hard times, the president reported to the board that Temple was looking for ways to properly position itself in "a very competitive market." One of the board members responded by saying that given Temple's difficulties, it had better increase its "sales budget." "An aggressive campaign to increase sales" could, he asserted, see the school through its difficulties. The president agreed. Another board member reminded the president that "our customer is the student" and Temple ought to do a better job of treating students as valued customers. The president responded to that assertion by saying that it always pained him when students were not thought of as "the most important commodity."[18]

In the early 1990s, there were three widely circulating homosexual newspapers in Philadelphia, as well as several gay and lesbian bookstores. One park was so gay-friendly that it was widely known as "Judy Garland Park." There was also a number of religious congregations in which lesbians and gays were welcome. However, there were only a few parts of the city where such couples could kiss in public without worrying about being subjected to violence.

During my fieldwork, Philadelphia was a violent city. In 1991, for instance, there were about 440 reported murders and about 900 reported rapes. In that same year there were about 13,000 reported robberies. To be sure, the statistics on violent crimes within the city did not look too bad when compared with those of the ten other largest cities in the United States. But when compared to cities in other countries, they looked awful, and, to me at least, the city often felt unsafe. Many places I walked or biked by regularly were sites of violence. In August 1992, a 70-year-old woman who lived on a block I knew well—a block only a five-minute walk from my apartment—was murdered. A friend of hers who lived a block south of my apartment was charged with the crime.

In December 1993, a man who was trying to hold up a coffee shop three or four blocks south of Oak Grove Church shot a man who interfered with the robbery; some of the field notes on which this book is based were written in that shop. In February of that year, a man who was attending church services several blocks southwest of the Philadelphia Mennonite Fellowship was shot to death.

The newspapers I read usually portrayed the various arms of the state as institutions that were attempting to contain and limit violence. Sometimes, however, they ran stories that hinted about how much of the state's activities involved the threat to employ—or did actually employ—violence to accomplish its ends. Some of the stories I clipped commented on the many federal jobs in Philadelphia that supported the U.S. military. Rather more stories described the violence Philadelphia police officers used in their efforts to keep the populace under control. That sort of violence was usually, but not always, presented in ways that made it appear natural and legitimate.

Philadelphia newspapers routinely ran stories about the city's efforts to recover from, or simply forget, the day that the city dropped a bomb on a house full of its own citizens. The bombing, part of the city's series of attempts to deal with a religiopolitical group called MOVE, took place in May 1985. It is not that long a walk from the building in which the Philadelphia Mennonite Fellowship met to the site of the bombing.

THREE

SOCIAL POWER

ASYMMETRICAL POWER

One matter in which religion and Philadelphia politics intersected in a particularly contentious way concerned how the city ought to treat same-sex couples. In 1996 the mayor of Philadelphia signed an executive order that extended city-paid health benefits to the domestic partners of a few of the lesbians and gay men who worked for the city. Mayor Rendell's order applied to only a handful of the city's employees. It would, he estimated, cost the city about $100,000 each year.

The leaders of a number of the city's churches found the mayor's executive order repugnant. One clergyman said that the order positioned the city to become the new Sodom and Gomorrah; another said that it might lead to the destruction of civilization. John Street—the president of the City Council—proclaimed that the mayor's order posed a dire threat to the social fabric of the city, and he then launched a campaign to prevent the order from ever taking effect. The campaign was, it seems clear, a genuine expression of Street's religious conviction. It might also have been an attempt to improve Street's relationship with the pastors of the city's Christian churches.

A few of the people on Philadelphia's City Council expressed their doubts about this negative campaign. One, a woman named Happy Fernandez, took particular issue with those men who argued that the domestic partnership order was a violation of biblical principles. "Throughout history, the Bible has been used to support a variety of destructive policies," Fernandez said. "White supremacists used the Bible to justify, first slavery, and later segregation and discrimination."[1]

In the 1980s and 1990s, such straightforward observations about the links between Christians' interpretation of the Bible and asymmetrical power relations were not made very frequently in Philadelphia's political circles.[2] But they were made quite frequently in the city's academic community and indeed throughout the national and international community of scholars. These observations deeply influenced my fieldwork. The portrait of Bible-carrying Christians that they embody is a common one in the world in which I live.

John Boswell, a student of the Middle Ages, reminded his readers, "From the fourteenth century on, Western Europe was gripped by a rabid and obsessive negative preoccupation with homosexuality as the most horrible of sins."[3] Cindy Patton, a young scholar who specialized in rhetoric and communications, asserted that Christians' interpretations of the Bible created a clear hierarchy between people with "normal" sex lives and those who did not adhere to biblical sexual norms:

> U.S. Protestantism is the heir of the Puritan notion that there is good sex and bad sex, good violence and bad violence. Good sex takes place in the confines of marriage and serves to weld together the family unit through procreation, or in the more liberal home, through the healthy display of intimacy within the married couple. Good violence is that exercised by the state through the military or police. The new right advocates penalizing non-marital, non-procreative sex with just violence—capital punishment, quarantine, or simply letting unrepentant homosexuals kill themselves off with AIDS.[4]

In academic communities, Christians' interpretations of the Bible were also routinely seen as contributing to the creation and maintenance of asymmetrical relations between women and men. Thus Donald Lowe, a historian of the modern United States, drew his readers' attention to the role that Christian churches (including some that were not made up of Bible-carrying Christians) had played in resisting moves toward less rigid and more symmetrical gender roles:

> Churches are fighting back with traditional arguments to shore up dichotomous gender attribution. Instead of recognizing that changes in gender construction are due to the hegemony of late-capitalist exchangist practices, they prefer to scapegoat "big government," feminists, liberals, and radicals for subverting dichotomous gender attribution. They insist that gender is

natural and universal, and therefore ought not to be tampered with. They appeal to the emotional ties people have invested in religious beliefs, and to a nostalgic, idealized past in order to shore up their argument.[5]

Academics often saw the Christian churches that made such arguments as organizations that carried within themselves a potent and disturbing set of authoritarian tendencies. In *Civil Society and Political Theory*, Jean Cohen and Andrew Arato asserted, for example, that "appeals to . . . tradition, religion, or community [can] foster the destructive fundamentalism of false communities [that is] easily manipulated from above."[6] A similar point was made by an Oxford theologian named Alister E. McGrath. He went so far as to compare the practices of some Bible-carrying Christian churches with the "priestcraft" against which Luther and Calvin had fought:

> The Reformation can be seen as a collective protest of the people of God against the errors, ignorances, and failures of their totalitarian ministers. But with the Reformation came a slogan— a slogan that needs to be splashed onto new banners again today: *ecclesia semper reformanda*—the church must always be reforming itself. In other words, reformation is not a once-and-for-all event, but a continuing process. Those who claim to stand in that evangelical tradition need to return to their roots and rediscover the need for continual correction, reform, and criticism of their ideas and actions.
>
> For the simple truth is that modern evangelicalism has spawned a number of ideas and attitudes that bear a disquieting resemblance to the worst excesses of the corrupt and confused church of the late Middle Ages.[7]

Such fears about "totalitarian ministers" and their capacity for mischief making were often conjoined with observations about the links between the power of Bible-carrying Christians and the power of for-profit corporations. Randall Balmer has pointed out, for example, the degree to which Bible-carrying Christianity has been organized and promulgated by such corporations.[8] Many social scientists have made the same point, and many of them have also emphasized the degree to which the votes of Bible-carrying Christians ended up serving the interests of large, multinational corporations.[9] The links between certain forms of Bible-carrying Christian churches and the peculiarly probusiness political culture of the United States in the Reagan years were an academic commonplace. "The most powerful capitalist nation in history," noted Terry Eagleton, a prominent literary theorist, was also a nation that had been decisively shaped by "a peculiarly noxious brand of Christian Evangelicalism."[10] Eagleton (and many other scholars) seemed to have been convinced that the links could not possibly be simply fortuitous.

Although academics were well aware of the fact that denunciations of "big government" and "the bureaucrats in Washington" could often be heard in Bible-carrying Christian churches, they also emphasized how patriotic such churches were.[11] Academics often pictured these churches as militant supporters of the interests of the American state. In Bible-carrying Christian churches, they suggested, a person who took a stand for Jesus Christ was, almost by definition, simultaneously taking a stand for the United States of America.[12]

Collectively, these paraphrases and quotations give us a sense of the general contours of an important and oft-told story about Bible-carrying Christians—the relationship between their churches and social power. This book is largely devoted to exploring the ways in which the narrative does and does not match what I saw and heard while doing my fieldwork.

This story (the one I am about to sketch) is extremely influential within some of the academic circles in which I move. It is the starting point from which many of my conversations with my students and my colleagues begin. For many of the people I talk to at Temple and in other academic settings, the narrative is almost self-evidently true.

It is not, of course, self-evidently true to me. If it were I would not have spent several years of my life investigating it. And there are things about this story (as will become clear shortly) that make me squirm with discomfort. But in relating it, I am not, by any means, simply creating a strawman. Even before I began my fieldwork, I was aware that there was a lot of evidence in the scholarly record that could be fit into the story quite nicely. More such evidence turned up nearly every day I was in the field.

Whatever else they are, the commonly accepted story begins, the congregations in which Bible-carrying Christians assemble are educational organizations. They are places where people are encouraged to accept a certain set of teachings about what the world is like and about how people should live their lives. Several observations about those stories can be advanced with great confidence.

First, these teachings emphasize the degree to which churches and families ought to be places where the authority and dominion of men over women is accepted and celebrated. Women who don't submit to male authority in the church and in the home are rebelling against God's will.

Second, these teachings also portray all those people who have sex with someone to whom they are not married as rebels against God. Men who have sex with other men and women who have sex with other women are violating God's fundamental laws; these sorts of violations are particularly unnatural and particularly repugnant. Bible-carrying Christian churches are, therefore, organizations where heterosexual norms are strictly enforced.

Third, the teachings that are promulgated end up by naturalizing the authority of Christian ministers. In Bible-carrying Christian churches, the members of the congregation are trained to think that it is natural for them to submit themselves to the authority of the man who serves as the pastor of their church. They are taught that in the end laypeople must submit to clerics. For this reason, these churches are best described as authoritarian rather than as democratic.

Fourth, the teachings that are promulgated do not really counteract the modern tendency of for-profit corporations to make all values and practices that contest their authority seem bizarre and unnatural. Instead, Bible-carrying Christian churches present God as a friend of business corporations. He is presented, too, as an opponent of organizations like unions and government branches that try to control the worst excesses of for-profit corporations.

The fifth (and final) generalization is closely related to the preceding observation. Given these churches' probusiness stances, their teachings almost inevitably include some rhetorical criticism of the various arms of the American state. But in such churches "big government" seldom includes the agencies of the American government that protect private property or that keep "illegal aliens" outside our nation's borders. Nor does "big government" often include the military or the domestic police. Bible-carrying Christians tend to support U.S. invasions of other countries; they tend to support the imprisonment of a large proportion of the American population.

So the denunciations of "big government" that one sometimes hears in such churches are not part of a general criticism of the way in which the American state tries to make all values and practices that contest its authority seem bizarre and unnatural. They are rather part of an attempt to say that one form of the modern nation-state (a form that resembles the sort found in Spain in the 1950s) is preferable to other forms (like those, for instance, in the Netherlands and in Sweden in the 1970s). Bible-carrying Christians are hostile to welfare states and to socialist ones. They are not, however, suspicious of the state per se.

AGENCY

Before proceeding, I want to note several peculiarities connected to these five observations. They seem to me to be based on the assumption that when one is analyzing Bible-carrying Christians, questions of power are absolutely crucial. They seem to bracket, or simply ignore, questions of truth and beauty.[13] Moreover, they do not pretend to give an objectively true description of what Bible-carrying Christians are really like. The observations are, rather, self-consciously partisan. They are expressed in idioms that are drawn from the feminist movements and from the gay and lesbian liberation movements and from American versions of the democratic, populist, anarchist, and Marxist traditions. The observations are not expressed in a way that attempts to minimize the tensions between these various political commitments and Bible-carrying Christians. Those tensions are, if anything, emphasized.

There is another peculiarity about the observations. They have a sort of shadow, a counternarrative that emphasizes the degree to which Bible-carrying Christian churches are places where people are "empowered" and where people are able "to exercise agency." This counternarrative, which has been told with some frequency in recent years, has now also become remarkably influential in the scholarly circles in which I move.[14] In fact, it is often seen as more interesting and more important than the story that emphasizes the links between domination and the churches associated with the New Christian Right.[15]

There are several different explanations for the counternarrative's growing appeal. For one thing, it accords well with scholars' tendency to present themselves as recusants. If "everybody knows" that Bible-carrying Christians churches are places where asymmetrical power relations prevail, some of us will be attracted to the idea of producing texts that explode "the conventional wisdom" about such churches. Then, too, many scholars are increasingly skeptical of *clear-cut* distinctions between those practices that are linked to asymmetrical power and those that are not. Few of us are willing to aver, for example, that the set of distinctions passed on to us from Marx or Locke still make perfect sense.

Moreover, some scholars are finding it increasingly difficult to ignore the similarities between the patronizing observations that are made about Bible-carrying Christians and colonizers' complaints about the flaws of "the primitive people," "the natives," and "the orientals" they encountered in the course of their conquests. These similarities make some of us nervous; they make us wonder whether a focus on the links between asymmetrical power and Bible-carrying Christians is helpful. Might not such a focus tend to give privilege to portrayals of Bible-carrying Christians that serve to legitimize those ways of looking at the world that are associated with well-to-do academics who have been deeply influenced by the European Enlightenment?[16]

I don't mean to imply that I began my fieldwork with a fixed hostility toward *all* the stories that scholars tell about the links between asymmetrical power and Bible-carrying Christianity. I did, however, view them with a good deal of suspicion. To me, they seemed too simple to do justice to the complexities of what my earlier research on the history of Bible-carrying Christianity had taught me, and they didn't seem to do justice to the complexities of these churches that I remembered from my childhood and early adolescence.

RETROSPECTION

Between 1957 and 1973, when I was growing up, I attended congregations in which it was assumed that people would carry their Bibles with them to church. Some of these congregations were in Alabama, others in desert towns in southern California. All of them were affiliated with the Southern Baptist Convention.

The pastors of our churches weren't called father; they were called brother. They were treated with respect, but they had very little *independent* authority. We believed in the priesthood of all believers. There was no sense in which pastors were priests in a way we were not. If pastors did things that we laypeople didn't like, they could be fired by a simple majority vote taken at any monthly business meeting.

Business meetings were run in an extraordinarily democratic manner. We believed in majority rule. Anything that smacked of "church hierarchy" was viewed with great suspicion. We Baptists were—at least when it came to church matters—deeply devoted to democracy. That was, we believed, one of the reasons that our churches conformed more closely to God's will than did the churches that Methodists and Presbyterians attended. They weren't democratic, and we were.

Only one of the members of my extended family ever gained enough fame in ecclesiastical circles to possibly merit even a passing mention in a published account of the history of the Southern Baptist Convention. Her name was Florence Thomasson. In my branch of the family, she was called Aunt Tommy. Aunt Tommy was one of the women who organized Southern Baptist "missionary unions" in the state of Alabama. Tommy never preached a sermon. She did, however, deliver lots of "talks" before churches. The difference between these talks of hers and the sermons that the men preached were sometimes not altogether clear.[17]

Tommy never married. Instead she established a household with her sister Nona, a beautiful woman who had been a missionary to China and who had spent several years in a Japanese war camp. To me, it was clear somehow that Nona was "wifely" and that Tommy was "husbandly." Tommy was not a lesbian and her relationship with Nona was sisterly, not homoerotic. But from the perspective of the 1990s, Tommy's life looks as if it departed in a number of important respects from the strictest bounds of American heterosexual norms. Yet, her way of life was never, as far as I can recall, criticized by anyone who attended a Southern Baptist church. Southern Baptists gave me the impression that they thought that Tommy's life was something that we Southern Baptists were proud of. That is, she embodied what it meant to be a good Southern Baptist.[18]

The churches I attended taught that a lot of behavior that "worldly people" thought was a mark of being "manly" was actually simply immoral. Christian men treated women with respect and love. They never acted like tyrants.

I recall my mother getting ready to go to one of the church's business meetings, which were held once a month. It had already been decided that she was going to denounce forcefully—ridicule even—some foolish action taken by the deacons. I don't recall what these men had done, but I do recall that my father's conversation with my mother about what she was going to say did not involve whether or not she was going to say it. That had already been decided, and my father had to admit that deacons often did foolish things. What he was hoping for—pleading for, I would say—is that my mother not denounce the deacons quite so forcefully as she had planned to, to tone things down a bit. My father would not have dreamed of trying to get her to give up her right to speak at a business meeting.

When I asked my mother if she could recall how the meeting turned out, she told me she couldn't. There were, after all, lots of times when she stood up and talked about some proposed action of the deacons that she thought was stupid. But my question did lead to another story. Sometime in the late 1960s or early 1970s, one of the deacons, a engineer named Mr. Hyche, launched a campaign to get me to cut my hair. The problem was this: he wanted his son, Dwight, to wear his hair short. His position was that wearing one's hair short was the appropriate thing for a young *Christian* man to do. One of the weaknesses in this argument—a weakness Dwight seems to have pointed out with some persistence—was that the church to which Mr. Hyche and Dwight belonged had a pastor, Ray Watt, whose son had shoulder-length hair. So pressure was brought to bear.

Long meetings were held between Mr. Hyche and the other deacons. Long meetings were held between Mr. Hyche and my father. Long meetings were held between Mr. Hyche and a visiting evangelist. (Mr. Hyche offered to pay him $100 if he could get me to cut my hair.) My mother found all these meetings outrageous. She told my father, and perhaps other people as well, that if my hair were cut she would never darken the church's doorway again as long as she lived. As things turned out, no one ever found out whether or not my mother was bluffing. My hair stayed long.

I greatly enjoy hearing this story. Like many other stories in my family, it reminds me of my mother's strength. Part of the pleasure also comes from the fact that I never knew anything about it at the time. Mr. Hyche might have teased me about my hair, but I never took him seriously. And neither my mother nor my father ever told me what Mr. Hyche and some of the other deacons were up to. I was insulated so completely from their plot that I did not learn of its existence until two decades after it had failed. In any case, my mother spoke often and well at the business meetings. I remember that the men in the congregation—most of whom were not as well educated or as articulate as she was—were a little afraid of her.[19]

Still, in the congregations I attended, women never preached, never presided over the Lord's Supper, and never baptized anyone. Indeed, they never even served as ushers. Women were taught that men were the head of the family. We knew what Paul had said about wives' being subject to their husbands, and we took it seriously.

We took our patriotism seriously, too. The American flag hung in the sanctuary of the congregations I attended as a child. During the summer those of us who were attending a set of summer classes called Vacation Bible School began each day with a procession. The American flag, along with the Bible and the Christian flag—a white and blue banner on which a cross had been imprinted—led the way. Almost as soon as the procession was over, we pledged allegiance to the Bible, to the Christian flag, and to the American one, although I cannot now recall in what order. I do recall that I never sensed any tension in pledging allegiance to the two flags. The two allegiances seemed seamless. And I do not think that any member of any the congregations that I attended between 1957 and 1973 ever seriously considered the possibility that Christianity and capitalism were in any real sense incompatible. Anticapitalists were communists; communists imprisoned Christians.

But that was not the whole story. We also had rituals that sacralized the community formed by our congregations. These rituals made this little community seem more real and more fundamental than the imagined communities that were associated with nation-states and with the "free enterprise system."

We were, for example, in the habit of singing a hymn called "Blest Be the Tie That Binds" at the end of every observance of the Lord's

Supper. At those times, the church building would be unusually quiet. We were singing a song in part because we believed that after the last supper they ate together, Jesus and his disciples sang a song before dispersing. Thus, we were imitating them. Believing that—believing that the singing was somehow tied up with the events that led up to Jesus' arrest—we tended to sing the song less exuberantly than most of the other songs we sang in church.

The words we sang were explicitly "Christian," and there was at least one explicit reference ("our Father") to God. The words focused, though, on the experience of belonging to a community in which hopes and sorrows were shared. It might be going too far to say that we worshiped that community, but we certainly revered it. We thought that the kingdom of God was among us. That community was never explicitly presented as being in opposition to the communities that were created by the state or by the free enterprise system. But it *was* presented—over and over again—as an alternative to them.[20]

But is *alternative* really the right word? On reflection, I am inclined to say no. It is not strong enough. The congregations I attended between 1957 and 1973 sometimes seemed to be claiming that the community to which "Blest Be the Tie That Binds" pointed was the *only* real community. The others were ephemeral. Their importance was downplayed, their pretensions deflated. They were not nearly so important as they pretended to be, and it would be a mistake, we knew, to take them too seriously.

FOUR

OAK GROVE CHURCH

HISTORY

Thomas S. Stuart's description and analysis of Oak Grove Church helped me to get my bearings there. He wrote "Fundamentalism, Americanism, and Culture" in 1994, when he was a practicing attorney. He was also a doctoral candidate in the Department of History at Temple University and had enrolled in a seminar I was leading on the history of religion in the United States.[1]

Stuart attended Oak Grove Church regularly when he was growing up and graduated from Oak Grove Christian Academy. At the time he wrote "Fundamentalism, Americanism, and Culture," he was chairman of the board that oversaw the academy but no longer regularly attended worship services at the church.

According to Stuart, the church was founded in 1931 and incorporated in 1944. The articles of incorporation declared that the purpose of the organization was "To provide and maintain a place of worship for its members to minister in the word, [and] to promote evangelism, at home and abroad."

For most of the history of Oak Grove, the people who lived in Olney were "white working-class Catholics." Beginning in the 1980s, the population of the neighborhood began to shift. A good number of Koreans, Latinos, and African Americans moved into Olney in the 1980s and 1990s. A few—not many—African Americans and Latinos have attended services from time to time at Oak Grove. And for many years a small but significant proportion of the church's membership has been made up of first-generation immigrants from the Ukraine and Brazil.[2]

Stuart's paper suggests that throughout its history Oak Grove has been a congregation made up overwhelmingly of people whose ancestors came to the United States from western Europe or the British Isles.

That was true in the early 1990s. It was even more true, the paper seems to suggest, in the preceding decades.

There was never a point in its history when Oak Grove Church was part of any tightly regulated denomination. From time to time, however, the church was associated with a group called the Independent Fundamental Churches of America. In Stuart's opinion, that group was "ultraconservative."

The history of the church was decisively shaped by a man named Paul Palmer. In Stuart's text, Palmer is described as "charismatic" and "occasionally domineering." Palmer worked as the pastor of Oak Grove for over thirty years. He retired shortly before I began my fieldwork at Oak Grove. When Palmer retired, a man who had been his assistant for decades—Phillip Foster—became the senior pastor. Palmer and Foster were both graduates of one of the most famous fundamentalist institutions in the United States: Bob Jones University. According to Stuart, Palmer and Foster "faithfully imparted" the fundamentalistic version of Christianity they learned at Bob Jones to the members of the church.

At Oak Grove, as at Bob Jones, women were given a good deal of advice about how they should act. They were, Stuart reports, "forbidden" to wear low-cut blouses or high-cut skirts. Such dress was thought to be "provocative." Moreover, women who wore slacks, pants, or shorts were viewed with a good deal of suspicion. Dressing in that way was thought to "endanger the marked distinction of the sexes . . . commanded by God in the Scriptures."

According to Stuart, wives at Oak Grove were taught that they had a duty to obey their husbands. Wives were taught, too, that they "should not work outside their homes." I cannot tell from the paper exactly what that injunction was taken to mean. Perhaps it meant no more than "in the best of all possible worlds, wives would not have to work outside the home." Perhaps it meant something more clear-cut. In any case, Stuart's paper makes it plain that many of the married women who attended church at Oak Grove did in fact work outside the home. It also points out that their doing so was sometimes motivated, at least in part, by a desire to find a way to pay for their children's tuition at the academy.

For much of its history Oak Grove Christian Academy had a formal, rigorous dress code. The code for girls specified that they could not wear shorts or slacks, and the hemlines of their dresses could not fall above their kneecaps. These rules were drawn up largely, Stuart's paper implies, because the people who ran the school did not want girls dressing in ways that might excite the "libido" of the boys who attended the school.

The code did not focus much on making sure that boys did not dress in ways that excited the female libido. It did specify, however, that their hair had to be cut short enough so that it did not touch their earlobes or their shirt collars. My hunch—it is little more than that— is that the people who drew up the codes thought that boys with long hair blurred the line between "masculine" and "feminine" in ways that were un-Christian.

Stuart's paper devotes a good deal of attention to the views of the people of Oak Grove toward the American government. They often seemed suspicious of—even hostile to—it. The most obvious example was, perhaps, Oak Grove Church's dissatisfaction with the public schools of Philadelphia. Indeed, Stuart says, the church established the academy, in 1968, largely because it wanted to prevent the state's schools from interfering with the efforts made by church members to instill a "fundamentalist worldview" in their children. The school was designed to make sure that the children of Oak Grove were never exposed to "the corrupting influences of public education."

In addition, Stuart notes that "many fundamentalists teach that the Social Security system is sinful, that the Federal Reserve System is sinful, that the income tax is sinful, etc." And, he adds, "Oak Grove has not been immune from some of these tendencies." At Oak Grove, welfare programs were particularly "suspect." They were seen as interfering with "the free market" and were thought to "encourage idleness." Moreover, they failed to do what the people at Oak Grove thought necessary: "punish" people who engage in immoral activity. Welfare programs were seen, therefore, as a particularly egregious example of a more general problem. According to Stuart, the people at Oak Grove Church believed that the American government had a "God-given duty to enforce morality" and that it had failed to discharge this duty. That failure was seen as catastrophic.

But Stuart's paper certainly does not indicate that the people who attended the church were uniformly hostile to the government of the

United States. Some passages make it clear that the people felt a strong attachment to the American government. Stuart recalled, for instance, that when he attended services there the auditorium of the church was "festooned with six or seven American flags." He could not recall any crosses being regularly displayed in the room. Also, the Oak Grove congregation thought of the American government as one that was founded by people just like them, that there was a sense in which the American government rightly *belonged* to people like them. Stuart reports that Oak Grove taught its members that America was "founded by fundamentalist Christians." Some speakers at the church even falsely claimed that "practically all of the signers of the Declaration of Independence were devout Christians [who were] persecuted by the English for their beliefs."

Stuart's paper has less to say than one might think about Oak Grove's involvement in partisan politics. It does, however, make a highly interesting point. Throughout much of the history of Oak Grove, members of the church were discouraged from participating in political coalitions (Moral Majority, for instance) that included people who were not fundamentalists because, Stuart believes, the church feared that such involvement "might lead to compromise." In the very recent past, however, that policy had changed. "Now," Stuart reports, "members are encouraged to enter the political realm whenever possible."

Although the church seems to have recently stepped up its political activities, some of its other activities may have become less vital. Church members' enthusiasm for Monday night visitation—a tradition that was aimed at winning converts for Christ—may well have declined somewhat in recent years.

Stuart's paper also reports that the cost of running Oak Grove's various activities has increased. The church's income, on the other hand, "has been steadily declining." The leaders of Oak Grove have responded to these pressures by "downsizing" the church. They have also responded—from time to time, at least—by denouncing those members of the church who do not give the church one-tenth of all their income. This failure to "tithe" is thought to be a sin, and people who commit that sin are accused of "robbing God."

A SAFE, FAMILIAR PLACE

I did not meet Thomas Stuart until my fieldwork was well underway. I myself have never been a member of a congregation associated with the New Christian Right, nor have I ever had much contact with such congregations, which do not get a lot of first-rate coverage in the newspapers I have read since coming to Philadelphia. So when I began the research project on which this book is based, I was unsure of how to go about getting in touch with such a congregation. I began by reading the work of students of religion in the United States.

One of the best ethnographies we have of Protestants in the contemporary United States is Susan D. Rose's 1988 *Keeping Them Out of the Hands of Satan*. The book focuses, in part, on the way a particular school educates its students. I learned a good deal from this book about an organization called Accelerated Christian Education, on which many schools associated with the New Christian Right have come to rely for help in figuring out what they should be teaching their children. Accelerated Christian Education encourages schools to adopt a form of instruction that is very tightly structured. The books it supplies to schools emphasize the virtues of free market economies. They teach traditional family values and stress the importance of becoming good patriots.

Thus, in January 1992, when I was looking for a fundamentalist church associated with the New Christian Right, I decided to find a church in Philadelphia that sponsored a school associated with Accelerated Christian Education.

As things turned out, it was not that hard to do. I got the number of the headquarters of Accelerated Christian Education, located in Lewisville, Texas. The person I spoke with there gave me the names of ten or so schools in the Philadelphia area that had some sort of affiliation with Accelerated Christian Education. Several of these schools were hard for me to contact: I couldn't find any trace of them in Philadelphia telephone directories. But the first school to which Accelerated Christian Education had directed my attention—Oak Grove Christian Academy—ran an ad in the yellow pages under "Schools—Private." It turned out that the school took its name from the congregation that sponsored it: Oak Grove Church.

Unless I have misremembered, the secretary whose phone rang when I called the number listed under Oak Grove Christian Academy also worked for Oak Grove Church. In any case, after making only one or two phone calls, I had been told that Oak Grove was associated with an assocation of fundamentalist churches and had been told, in a welcoming voice, when the church's Sunday School classes and worship services took place.

Both the church and the school were located in a neighborhood in Philadelphia called Olney. Early in the course of my fieldwork, I arranged to have an Episcopal priest, Mary Ludlow, take me on a tour of the neighborhood. Ludlow had grown up near Oak Grove Church and was now the vicar of an Episcopal church in Olney. That church and the church where I worshiped worked together to raise money to fund a summer camp for children.

There were, Ludlow said, lots of drugs and some streetwalkers in Olney, and many of the people who lived there wanted to move elsewhere. A huge set of warehouses that had been run by Sears and had provided a lot of jobs had been shut down in the recent past, as had the Heinz factory (which made machines, not ketchup). There was still a Kardon auto parts plant in the area, but, Ludlow said, the working conditions were bad and the pay was poor.

Whenever I drove between the building in which the church held its worship services and the building in which Oak Grove Academy held its classes, I went past a naval supply depot and a plant owned by Mrs. Paul's Kitchens, both of which were on the verge of closing. I got the impression that the church building had been vandalized more than once, but not the building where the academy held its classes. However, the school building looked a little like a fortress, and its windows were covered with wire mesh. From time to time, I heard or read stories about brutal crimes that had been committed in the immediate vicinity of either the school or the church.

In part perhaps because their church was located in a neighborhood that contained few people who were wealthy, the men who delivered sermons at Oak Grove did not have many good things to say about the rich. Rich people, they said, tended to live lives that made it hard for them to come to a saving knowledge of Christ, whereas poor people tended to live in a manner that brough them closer to God. Poor people were, in fact, described in ways that seemed to suggust that God loved them more passionately than he loved those who were rich.

Sermons preached at Oak Grove asserted that God had a particular interest in making sure that the physical needs of poor were met. Jesus was said to have evinced a particular concern for the needs of the poor; followers of Jesus were obliged to do the same. Preachers at Oak Grove told their hearers that Christians had a God-given obligation to take practical steps to help the poor. Christians who failed to meet that obligation were sinning grievously and would have to answer for that sin before the judgment seat of God.

Sermons at Oak Grove also asserted that Christians who ministered to the needs of the poor but were reluctant to encourage poor people to actually become members of their own congregation were rebelling against God's commands. There was no warrant, preachers said, for running a church in any way that discriminated against the poor. Christians who did so were simply refusing to adhere to the word of God.

When I drove or walked toward the buildings owned by Oak Grove Church, the streets usually seemed empty and forbidding. The buildings themselves, however, were often full of activity and felt safe. Basketball was being played, hymns were being sung, prayers were being said, and children were getting lots of attention from adults.

Also, the buildings Oak Grove owned were places where people could talk about their lives and be sure that they would be taken seriously. Men and women who were ill could go there and pray for help. So could immigrant families who were having difficulty making a life for themselves in the United States or people who were afraid they were about to lose their jobs. Married couples who had been separated could come to Oak Grove and ask God to strengthen their marriage. People with AIDS could come and ask for God's help, too. Oak Grove felt like a safe place, like a refuge from the lonely (and somewhat unsafe) streets of Olney.

I first attended services at Oak Grove Church on February 9, 1992. It was a cold, windy day, probably in the 20s, but it was also sunny. I took a city bus to the Broad Street subway and then took the subway up to the corner of Roosevelt Boulevard and Broad. I walked from there to the church (perhaps a twenty-minute walk). In a way, going to this church felt a little like going home. Oddly enough, the first man I spoke to after walking in the door had the same name as my father and grandfather: Ray Watt. Ray Watt and I could not find any common relatives. His folks are from New Jersey. My father's are from Virginia and, before that, from Iowa. And certainly we did not look anything alike: he was about 60, short and thin and hawk-nosed and dark; I was 35, tall, 190 pounds, and quite pale. Still, for a minute I thought I had stumbled into a world of magic realism.

And the church felt familiar. The building was built in 1963 out of stone. It reminded me in a vague way of many Southern Baptist churches I have known. The Christian flag was on the left of the sanctuary, the American on the right. I had seen similar arrangements before. The table for the Lord's Supper said: "Do this in remembrance of me." That seemed familiar, too.

The table was overshadowed by the pulpit. Behind the pulpit was a choir, which seemed to include about twice as many women as men. Behind that was the baptistery. The people seemed a little tense and not very joyous. The songs were ones I knew, some of them my favorites. The doxology that had begun every Sunday morning service I had attended as a child was woven into a song the choir sang in a way that I thought was beautiful. We sang the doxology, the choir sang something more complicated, and the two songs melded well. I realized that I was beaming.

At the last minute the leaders of the service switched from a hymn that was listed in the bulletin to "Joyful, Joyful, We Adore Thee." That was Beatrice Watt's favorite hymn (Beatrice Watt was married to my grandfather, Ray Watt, Sr.) and it had been sung at her funeral. (Actually "An die Freude," it is one of few pieces of classical music I heard during my childhood.) And I loved reading antiphonally from the twelfth chapter of Romans. The passage we read was taken from the King James Version. On some level I must believe that this is the way Scripture should sound; any other way seems to me to be too modern and too flat.

Jane Thomas, one of the members of Oak Grove interviewed by my colleague Pam Hayden, said that although she believed that the Bible stated that homosexuality was wrong and that she herself felt "uncomfortable" around lesbians, she also believed that homosexuals should not be condemned for their sexual orientation. It was not, she said, something that they had chosen for themselves, so it was inappropriate for

Christians to condemn them. She herself talked about homosexuality and about related issues in ways that led Hayden to conclude that she was a "compassionate" person, a person who was extremely reluctant to judge others harshly.

However, it would be difficult to describe the leaders of Oak Grove as feminists, although some sermons did claim that there was a great deal of tension between Christian ideals about how families should be run and kinship structures that give fathers and husbands too much authority over their daughters and wives.[3] Some of the members of the church, moreover, concluded that it was wrong for wives and husbands to concentrate too much on the biblical passage that talks about a woman's duty to submit to her husband's authority (Ephesians 5.22) They had come to believe that women and men "are equal in God's eyes" and ought therefore to also "be equal" in the home that they had established together.[4]

At Oak Grove, women had less influence on shaping worship services and administering church finances than men did. But women sometimes did give brief and informal talks during Oak Grove's Sunday services, and they did speak with some frequency and with a good deal of eloquence during the Wednesday night prayer meetings. They also had a good deal of authority in running the church's finances. For example, they had been given—or perhaps had simply assumed—more or less complete control of the $5,000 or so the church spent each month to meet its "commitment to missionaries."[5]

Dangers associated with the world of business received a lot of attention in the sermons preached at Oak Grove. If a man was looking for "integrity," he would be a fool to try to find it in the "corporate world." Men who allowed themselves to get caught up in climbing the corporate ladder were likely to do *irreparable* harm to themselves and their families. Preachers particularly denounced the materialism and greed that they associated with the world of American businessmen. They told their listeners that Americans have a tendency to "worship" work and money. Doing so, they said, "gets our eyes off God" and "leads to captivity."

"Cultural captivity" was a condition that was viewed with great suspicion at Oak Grove. Sermons repeatedly emphasized the importance of "not being conformed to the world." They argued that Jesus had clearly denounced and challenged "the system of his day" and that followers of Jesus in the contemporary United States had to do the same thing. They had to realize that they were living in the midst of a system that is "crooked and perverse" and that "Christians are called to live apart from [such a] system."[6]

This criticism of "cultural captivity" was echoed in the literature that Oak Grove distributed to its members. A remarkable article by Steve Stohler, "The Evangelical Subculture," is a good case in point. It consistently emphasizes the gulf between "the value system of our surrounding culture" and the values to be found in the Sermon on the Mount and in the other teachings of Jesus. The article, which draws on the arguments of Christian writers such as Jim Wallis, John Alexander, and Jacques Ellul, asserts that Jesus' values were "radically countercultural" and stresses the need for Christians to live their lives according to Jesus' values rather than those of "the prevailing American culture."[7]

The worship services at Oak Grove were often run in ways that underscored the church's attachment to the doctrine of the priesthood of all believers. On Wednesday nights, for instance, the service proceeded without reference to any formal printed order of worship. Those in attendance sometimes decided which songs to sing by calling out in turn page numbers from the church's hymnal. And on Wednesday nights we sometimes decided which prayers to pray by simply arranging ourselves into a half dozen or so small circles, letting the other people in our circle know what was "on our hearts" that evening.

However, our praying and singing was not by any means *entirely* free from ministerial authority. If someone had requested "Ninety-nine Bottles of Beer on the Wall" rather than one of the songs in the hymnal, the minister would have politely made sure that didn't happen. He would no doubt also have stepped in if he had happened to hear someone in a prayer circle ask us to pray for the Socialist party to triumph in the national elections. But the minister certainly did not dictate the service, and the service did not indicate that the people at Oak Grove wanted their ministers to control the way in which God is worshiped.

ASYMMETRIES

Nevertheless, I often felt that the leaders of both Oak Grove Academy and Oak Grove Church believed that "submission to authority"—

especially submission to the authority of a minister of the gospel, such as Pastor Foster—was a good thing. I also felt that many of the students at the academy and nearly all the members of the church shared that belief.

The authority Foster exercised rested in part on being seen (to borrow a phrase from a guest speaker) as the "commander in chief." The people at Oak Grove really did believe that they were involved in a series of pitched battles against the world, the flesh, and the devil. They were genuinely grateful for the leadership Foster provided in that struggle.

Foster's authority rested, too, on his role as a sort of chief executive officer. The bylaws of Oak Grove Church, a copy of which I obtained in the course of my fieldwork, gave an enormous amount of power to the senior pastors and his closest advisers. The bylaws provided for an annual meeting that sounded a good deal like an annual stockholders' meeting, but they seemed to place more day-to-day power in an "Official Board" that was chaired by the senior pastor. The bylaws seemed to ensure that most of what happened at Oak Grove Church would be under his surveillance.

Foster's authority also rested on his routinely presiding over the Sunday morning worship services, which lasted well over an hour. Ten minutes or so of the service was routinely given over to announcements by Foster and to prayers that he offered to God. About thirty minutes was scheduled for the sermon, which was usually, though not always, delivered by Foster himself. When other men preached, I got the impression that they knew that if they said things Foster found objectionable, they would not be invited to preach again.

Indeed I got the impression that very little, if anything, could happen at a public worship service without Foster's approval. The men on the podium and the men and women in the choir were not likely to do anything that did not meet with his approval, and no else in the room could do very much to shape the service. They could join in the recitation of a particular passage of Scripture and in the singing of particular hymns, but the hymns and scriptural passages had been chosen beforehand and printed in the bulletin. They were not going to be negotiated.

I don't mean to say that the Sunday morning worship services were poorly run. They were, in fact, run quite well. The music sometimes struck me as quite fine, and the sermons nearly always were extra-ordinarily thoughtful and well delivered. But the Sunday morning services were run in such a way that it was clear that Foster was very much in control of Oak Grove Church.[8]

His authority also rested on his serving as the congregation's chief biblical interpreter. Foster's sermons always took the form of a careful explication of biblical passages. The passages to which he directed his auditors' attention were marked as especially important. His interpretations were clearly informed by some knowledge of Greek and by certain strands within the tradition of Protestant biblical scholarship; they seemed to have been regarded by the members of Oak Grove as both "learned" and "authoritative."

The people at Oak Grove Church and Oak Grove Academy seemed to believe that "obedience to the [civil] government" is one of the more important duties of a Christian.[9] That obedience was, in most cases, given quite cheerfully. The people I met at Oak Grove were deeply patriotic. They loved the United States of America and found attacks on it—like those made by some leftists in the 1960s and 1970s—deeply distressing. They were "shocked" by Americans who were willing to "denigrate their own country."[10] They were also shocked by the decision some American men made in the 1960s and 1970s to refuse "to serve their country" in the armed forces in Indochina.[11]

In part, perhaps, because they wanted to see to it that the children of Oak Grove never made such ungodly decisions, the leaders made patriotic songs and rituals a part of the routine at the academy. The academy sponsored concerts that were devoted largely—exclusively, even—to music that was explicitly patriotic, and the chapel services at the academy included the pledge of allegiance to the American flag.

Moreover, the leaders of Oak Grove made sure that patriotic rites were sometimes incorporated into the church's own Sunday morning services. On June 14, 1992, for example, the church observed Flag Day. On that occasion, the sanctuary was festooned with no fewer than six American flags; they seemed to overwhelm the symbols that were explicitly tied to the Christian faith. At one point in the service, all the members of the congregation pledged their allegiance to the flag. The recitation was led by twenty or so boys and men dressed in uniforms, which were olive and brown and decorated with red, white, and blue patches—imitations of or perhaps tributes to the uniforms worn by members of the American military services.[12]

The patriotic rituals I observed at Oak Grove were not, of course, intended to show that a Christian's allegiance to the American flag should be greater than his or her allegiance to the Christian flag or to the Bible. That wasn't the point. Part of what made the rituals so striking was the way in which they seemed to assure the people who took part that there was no fundamental tension between the American state and the kingdom of God. The rituals seem to imply that one of the best ways for Christians to express their loyalty to the kingdom of God was to stand up for America. The rituals seemed to rest on the assumption that it made little sense to try to distinguish too sharply between one's loyalty to the kingdom of God and one's loyalty to the American state. The two citizenships were presented, rather, as mutually reinforcing.[13]

Some of the sermons I heard at Oak Grove seemed to rest on the same assumption. At least one of them began with a focus on the importance of gaining citizenship in the kingdom of God, and it ended with stories of an American citizen who lectured taxi drivers and soldiers in the Middle East about their lack of respect for the United States. The point of the sermon seemed to be that any good American Christian would want to stand up for America whenever one could. A failure to do so might be interpreted, I gathered, as a sign of spiritual weakness.

The pastor of Oak Grove, Phillip Foster, was among many other things a man who enjoyed looking for shrewd financial investments. In the course of our conversations, I got the impression that he was pretty good at doing that. He told me, for instance, that a land investment he had made in a part of California where I had lived in the late 1960s and early 1970s, Antelope Valley, had paid off handsomely. By the time he sold it, the land was worth something like $140,000.[14] And by the time that I concluded my fieldwork, Foster owned part of a company that stood a chance, he thought, of making something like $125 million in the next few years.

So there is, then, a sense in which asking whether "members of the business classes" had decisively shaped the way in which Foster viewed the world is a good deal like asking whether "Roman Catholics" decisively influenced the views of John Paul II and Mother Teresa. Foster *was*, in fact, a member of the business classes, as were a great many of the other leaders of Oak Grove.

The man who preached a guest sermon during Missions Emphasis Week at Oak Grove—a man from Haiti who was hostile to liberation theology and Aristide—was, for example, an entrepreneur, as well as a preacher. The factory that he and his brother ran in Haiti employed about 100 people. The man who oversaw my visits to Oak Grove Academy, Bob DiFranco, was also a businessman. I believe that DiFranco had made enough money from his real estate business to be set for life and no longer needed to work for a living.

Although I did not learn very much about the board that oversaw Oak Grove Academy during the course of my fieldwork there, my conversations with DiFranco convinced me that the board—which had once included a number of people who were blue-collar workers—was now increasingly dominated by professionals and businessmen. The board members now, DiFranco told me, knew how to run things in a business-like way. Each of the businessmen and professionals on the board was the sort of man who could bring in $10,000 worth of gifts from friends and acquaintances every year. Some of them could afford to simply write out a check to the school for that amount whenever they needed to.

During one of my visits to Oak Grove Academy, DiFranco asked me several questions about my project. As I was answering, I talked—for a just moment or two, as I recall—about the relationship between religious institutions and the marketplace. That was the part of my answer that seemed to spark the most interest. It raised some issues about which DiFranco had reached a definite conclusion. He told me, with a good deal of confidence and a certain amount of eagerness, that it was clear to him that religious institutions in the contemporary United States had no choice but to accommodate themselves to the realities of the marketplace.

When the school began, DiFranco said, it had been hoped that the board of trustees, the administrators, the faculty, *and the students* would all be fundamentalists. That had not happened. Instead, the students came from families who attended a wide array of Protestant churches, including evangelical or pentecostal ones. Some even attended churches that were associated with the National Council of Churches, which has long been *the* bête noire of many fundamentalists.

So the student body at Oak Grove had become a good deal less fundamentalistic than the founders of the school hoped it would be. That was not the result, DiFranco made clear, of the leaders of Oak Grove Academy making a principled decision to embrace ecumenism. It had happened, rather, because the leaders of the school knew that they had to accommodate themselves to the realities of the market. They knew that there were relatively few fundamentalist families in the neighborhoods near Oak Grove Academy who were able to pay the sort of tuition the school had to charge to meet its expenses. They knew that if the school tried to draw its students exclusively from such families, it would have to close its doors. Not wanting to see that happen, the leaders of Oak Grove had reached out to families that were not fundamentalistic. Thus, religious principle had to give way to the realities of the market.

The textbooks used by students at the academy did not encourage the possibility that religious institutions in the United States could, or should, resist such an accommodation. In fact, the curriculum—a good deal of which was produced by Accelerated Christian Education—suggested that there was little or no tension between free market principles and the Christian way of life. The leaders of the academy presumably thought that there was nothing at all odd about a company making a profit by selling a curriculum designed to help boys and girls mature into devout Christian adults. And there was no suggestion that there might be any tension between a healthy respect for the institution of private property and loyalty to the kingdom of God. Rather, everyone who taught or studied at Oak Grove Academy was expected to appreciate the importance of property rights, and those who failed to do so enraged the leaders of the school.[15]

Students were also expected—or perhaps *encouraged* is the better word—at least to consider pursuing a career in business. A voluntary association that taught high school students how to become successful entrepreneurs was given access to Oak Grove's students, who were encouraged to see that mastering such entrepreneurial skills might enable them to make a valuable contribution to American society, as well as to win financial security for themselves and their families.

No sharp line was drawn between the world of commerce and the world of religion at Oak Grove Academy. Indeed, there was hardly any demarcation at all between them. The situation was similar at the church.

Because it was so pervasive, the intermingling of commerce and religion eventually lost its novelty. I almost stopped noticing it.

But when my friend Bruce Comens visited the church with me, he was struck by how much its life seemed to be dominated by commerce. The essay he wrote afterward—"The Business of Belief"— asserted that the church presented "an astonishing amalgam of Christianity [and] capitalism." In fact, Comens thought that the people at Oak Grove believed that capitalism, as it was expressed in the contemporary United States, was something close to an earthly embodiment of "the heavenly kingdom."[16] It seemed clear to Comens that the unreflective "use of metaphors drawn from capitalism" was absolutely "fundamental to the imaginative structuring of the religion" that was practiced at Oak Grove. The church's pastor looked and talked like a businessman, and the sermon Foster preached sounded a lot like "a sales pitch."[17]

On my earliest visits to the Oak Grove, I, too, was struck by the way in which commerce and religion were intertwined. On one of my first visits, for example, I was surprised when the church gave me something that reminded me of products given away by insurance agents: an inexpensive ballpoint pen printed with the church's name and address. All visitors to Oak Grove were given a similar pen.

Also, the first time I attended a Sunday School class, I was struck by how much it seemed to have been influenced by practices borrowed from corporations. The class was devoted to helping the people discover what "spiritual gifts" God had blessed them with and what they ought to be doing to use those gifts for God's service. Our spiritual gifts, it turned out, could be measured in much the same way that the resources of a particular employee could be measured by a skillful manager in the personnel department. All we had to do was complete a standardized test given to the class by the leader. We filled in little circles that signaled our answers to a set of questions about what sort of activities we found enjoyable. The class was assured that, properly understood, determining one's spiritual gifts was no more difficult than going to McDonald's.[18]

From time to time in the course of my fieldwork, people asked me about my private life. Because I answered truthfully, some people at Oak Grove knew that I was divorced, that I was dating a woman who was slightly older than I was, and that she had an 11-year-old daughter. No one ever asked me directly whether I was sleeping with this woman. If anyone had, I would have told the truth. The answer would have displeased people at Oak Grove, and most of them would have been willing to say that my divorce violated biblical principles. But the way I was living my life was something they could recognize and respond to. It did not make me so different from them that communication was impossible. It did not make me the sort of person they could not in good conscience allow to do fieldwork in their congregation. In fact, on numerous occasions they went out of their way to help me.

However, an uncloseted lesbian or gay man who tried to do the same fieldwork would almost certainly have been treated less kindly. It might even have been impossible—or at least next to impossible—for such a person to do so because both the church and academy were places where heterosexual norms were enforced with a good deal of strictness and a great deal of passion. They were not places where people who questioned these norms were treated with much charity. A gay fieldworker would have encountered a great deal of suspicion and hostility.

Once, when I was at the church, Foster waved me into his office and we spoke for thirty minutes or so. With no prompting whatsoever, he told me about the sermon he had preached on the previous Sunday. It was partly concerned with a homosexual couple who had mixed their sperm together and used the mixture to impregnate a woman.[19] (Foster had seen this story on the Cable News Network.) He found this story enraging, offensive, and disgusting, partly, I knew, because he believed that homosexuality is "unbiblical." But I thought the rage was too great to be explained simply on the basis of what the Bible has to say about which sexual practices are proper and which are not.

It occurred to me that I had known few people in my life more choleric than Foster. It also occurred to me that I found it unusually difficult to respond to his remarks about homosexuals. On nearly all the occasions on which I disagreed with the people I met at Oak Grove, I could find some common ground on which we could continue to talk. I could not do so on this occasion. I suspected that in Foster's mind the starting point for a conversation would have to be the loathsomeness of homosexuality. If we were in agreement about that, more could then be said. If not, there was nothing to talk about.

On another day, at the academy, I observed a sixth-grade class taught by Gloria Burke, a kind and intelligent woman who was perhaps in her late 50s. In the course of the day, she led a discussion on a bill that was being considered in the state capital that would affect the way Pennsylvania educates its children. As she was speaking, she casually said: "We are against gay people." Later she said: "Of course, we still love them [gay people]." At the time, I thought it possible that the additional remark was made for my benefit and that if I had not been in the room nothing would have been said about "love."[20]

At Oak Grove, I often got the impression that women were second-class citizens.[21] The bylaws of the church prohibited women from serving on the official board, and the leaders of the church thought that ordaining a woman as either a deacon or a pastor was unthinkable. Indeed, except in a very few circumstances, women were expected to keep silent in the church on Sunday mornings. I once heard a woman deliver a very brief "testimony," and I once heard a woman answer a question that the pastor asked about her husband's health. Other than that, I don't think I ever heard a woman, speaking as an individual, say anything at all during a Sunday morning service.[22]

Neither I nor any of my research assistants ever met a woman at the church or academy who had decided she would rather be called *Ms.* than *Miss* or *Mrs.* And when I slipped and called women Ms. Jones or Ms. Smith rather than Mrs. Jones or Mrs. Smith, my mistake was noted and corrected. Nor did we ever hear people at the church or academy describe themselves as feminists. We did, however, hear a good deal of explicit condemnation of feminism, some of which was impassioned enough to make us uncomfortable. One of the interviews Hayden conducted with Susan Bateson, for example, left Hayden feeling "disturbed":

> This interview was tougher for me. We discussed gender roles, and I found myself personally almost nauseated at some of the things she said about women. I tried to remain as neutral as I could in body language and tone; certainly I didn't give myself

away verbally. I cognitively knew that fundamentalists take an extremely conservative, right-wing view politically; I don't think personally I've heard another women articulate the same rhetoric as the male politicians and preachers who are so blatantly anti-feminist. It was as though she was parroting what her pastor and husband said about women, and she agreed with it."[23]

FIVE

THE PHILADELPHIA MENNONITE FELLOWSHIP

LIVING WITH INTEGRITY

Oak Grove, then, was a place where women were not allowed to preach and where most of the positions of authority were monopolized by men. It was also a place where modern feminism was seen as profoundly incompatible with biblical Christianity. Things were quite different at the second church in which I did my fieldwork: the Philadelphia Mennonite Fellowship. Here, the congruence between "authentic Christianity" and certain forms of feminism was repeatedly emphasized. Women always served on all of the congregation's important committees, and women frequently delivered sermons at the Sunday morning worship services. But the Philadelphia Mennonite Fellowship was also a place where masculine authority was sometimes reinforced. It was a congregation, for example, in which people seemed to assume that the sovereign of the universe was masculine rather than feminine and that informal Bible study groups ran most smoothly when the men sat in chairs and the women sat on the floor.

But I did not learn that until my fieldwork was well underway. All I knew at first was that the fellowship a practiced with enthusiasm and zeal a particular variety of Bible-carrying Christianity—one that is in many ways well to the left of American liberalism.

In December 1991, I called Ron Sumner, a professor at Eastern Baptist Theological Seminary, a school just outside of Philadelphia that was affiliated with the American Baptist Convention. I knew of him because he was one of the founders of Evangelicals for Social Action. I sketched out my research project and told him that I wanted an evangelical church that did not assume that the will of God was perfectly congruent with the needs of modern corporations or modern nation-states. Did he know, I asked, of any such churches in the Philadelphia area? Sumner thought for a moment or two and then suggested the Philadelphia Mennonite Fellowship.

On January 3, 1992, I called David Geist, the pastor of the Philadelphia Mennonite Fellowship, to ask him when and where his congregation held its worship services. He told me 10:30 on Sundays in a building near the University of Pennsylvania. I said I'd like to attend services the next Sunday. As things turned out, someone other than Geist was scheduled to preach that particular Sunday. And it seemed to me that Geist thought it might make sense for me to save my first visit for a day when he was preaching. Thus my initial visit to the Philadelphia Mennonite Fellowship didn't occur—as I had planned—on the day before Epiphany, but instead, on January 12.

During our first phone conversation, Geist and asked whether I was the same David Watt who had recently published a review in the *Evangelical Studies Bulletin*. The *Bulletin*, a journal with a tiny circulation list made up mostly of people with a scholarly interest in the history of evangelicalism in the United States, had indeed recently published my article, "Evangelicalism, the Market, and the State in Nineteenth-Century America." It focused on sociological works that emphasized the plutocratization and the commercialization of nineteenth-century evangelical churches,[1] suggesting that those processes were near the heart of the history of evangelicalism in North America. As far as I could tell, Geist had never read or even seen anything else that I had written, and no other member of the church had ever seen *anything* that I had written. Still, I had hoped for a more anonymous beginning.

On January 12, 1992, I began fieldwork at the Philadelphia Mennonite Fellowship.[2] The service started at 10:30 and was followed by a fellowship meal and by a congregational meeting to discuss the annual budget. The meeting did not conclude until 3:10 or so. The room in which the meal and the two meetings took place looked a little like an assembly room in a junior high school. The ceiling was low, the decoration minimal. There was nothing about it that struck me as particularly "ecclesiastical."

The Philadelphia Mennonite Fellowship did not own the building in which it held its meetings. The building was owned by a school whose theological position was fairly conservative: the Philadelphia Theological Seminary of the Reformed Episcopal Church. The school charged the congregation for the use of its property.

Although the neighborhood was just a few blocks north of one of the nation's most prestigious and expensive universities, it was not, by any stretch of the imagination, a prosperous one. There was a lot of trash on the block where the congregation met, and at least one of the buildings was boarded up. On the boards someone had written such phrases as "The blood of Jesus Christ, God [sic] Son washes away all sins," and "Believe on the Lord Jesus and thou shall be save" [sic]. One of the parking lots on the block was protected by a high fence topped with a spiral of barbed wire.

I found it hard to make more than a few generalizations about the people at the service. There were some people of color. One family seemed to be from the Indian subcontinent, and one woman was from the Far East. There were several blacks, too; some might have been Africans rather than African Americans. But most of the people at the church were white.

Many of the men had beards, one that reached almost to the man's navel. No one was particularly fashionable. There were lots of couples. Some of the people looked like undergraduates, some like graduate students. Many appeared to be in their late 30s and early 40s. the mean age might have been 32.

Nearly all of the people I heard speak and nearly all of the people I talked to informally seemed highly intelligent. Some were studying to become lawyers, teachers, physicians, ministers, social workers, or professors. Some had already finished their studies and had started working in their professions. It seemed that many people there were trying to make a living by doing good.

The worship service itself lasted about ninety minutes. It included a few elements—such as following a lectionary and taking note of holy days like Epiphany—that I associated more with Lutheran and Anglican liturgies than with traditional Mennonite worship services. On the whole, however, the service was remarkably informal and was largely led by the laity. People clapped from time to time, and the songs were generally quite simple. Indeed, the service as a whole was simple rather than baroque. It struck me, accustomed as I was to the rituals of the Episcopal Church, as almost aesthetically impoverished. It seemed to be *too* low church, *too* plain.

No offering plate was passed; instead, a box was placed at the back of the room. People who wanted to give money to the church had to go a little out their way to do so. Several members of the congregation have said, I learned later, that they would leave the congregation if it started passing a plate.[3]

In one portion of the service—"thanksgiving and concerns"—people in the congregation stood up and talked about what was going on in their lives and the lives of those around them. Another portion was set aside for people to respond to, ask questions about, and even take issue with the sermon. Another portion—the very end—provided time for everyone in the congregation to form themselves into a circle, join hands, and say a prayer.

The sermon was impressive. I have heard many good sermons in my life, and I have very little patience for those that are boring or ill prepared. But even after Geist had been preaching for twenty-five minutes, I found myself hoping, as my notes record, that he would keep preaching. I found what he was saying to be interesting and I didn't want him to stop. The main point of the sermon grew out of Geist's insistence that the Christians who lived during the New Testament era and the Anabaptists who lived in the sixteenth century both lived lives that possessed a great deal of integrity. The question to which he directed the congregation's attention was how can we—meaning both "all Christians who are alive today" and "the people in this room"—live with as much integrity as did those two groups of saints. Geist did not suggest that if people followed some seven-step formula their lives would possess integrity, nor did he say that we should simply mimic past generations of saints. Instead he tried to prod people into systematically reflecting on a question to which (he seemed to assume) no one could give a simple answer.

After the service ended, people began setting up for the potluck supper. I hadn't known there was going to be one, so I hadn't brought any food. Nevertheless, people encouraged me to stay and I didn't feel at all uncomfortable doing so. The food was not fancy, but there was plenty of it and much of it was good. It was the sort of food that you could cook with the recipes in the *More-with-Less Cookbook*: the sort that might be prepared by people who wanted to avoid "eating high on the food chain." After the supper everybody pitched in to clean up and to put the chairs and tables back in their original places.

Then the congregational meeting began, one that was mostly concerned with money. The general quality of the discussion was remarkably high and the people were extremely articulate. They also struck me as possessing all sorts of arcane knowledge. One person knew, for instance, the precise denominations in which certificates of deposit may be purchased. I couldn't have told you that to save my life.

Before the meeting was over, a new annual budget had been approved. But that had not happened without a good deal of tension and conflict. Two separate issues seemed to cause concern. First, some people at the meeting felt that the congregation as a whole had not been given enough input into the budget process. The people who drew up the budget were told in so many words that the opportunities for such input were "less than adequate." They were told—again in so many words—that things should be different next year.

The second issue was the salary and benefits given to David Geist, which several members of the congregation thought were too high. That surprised me. Geist had an earned doctorate. His salary for the previous year was $32,000, and under the proposed budget he would be given a $2,000 raise. To me, $34,000 did not seem like a high salary in a city as expensive to live in as is Philadelphia.[4] But some of the people argued that Geist's salary was considerably higher than the average salary in the congregation. Some even noted that there was some tension between Mennonite customs and paying a minister any money whatsoever.

The discussion of the salary issue was not rancorous; it was bracketed by several observations about what a good job Geist was doing. Still, it struck me as remarkably egalitarian. Geist sat silently in the pew while the congregation talked for twenty minutes or so about whether or not his salary was, as someone put it, too "hefty." It is hard to imagine the president of Temple University enduring a faculty meeting in which his salary—which was, I would guess, about 800 percent heftier than Geist's—was debated. Certainly the faculty at the school would never allow their students to debate and decide their salaries.

Geist sent me a note a few days after my first visit to his church. Although it was written on stationery printed with the fellowship's name and address, the note was not at all ostentatious. It was written by hand with a blue pen in letters that hovered between cursive and print. The printed material that accompanied the note looked as though it had been prepared on an old typewriter and a cheap mimeograph machine.

[Philadelphia Mennonite Fellowship]
[David Geist], Pastor

7777 Chestnut Street
Philadelphia, PA 19177
(215) 777–7777

Dear David,

It was good having you in worship with us last Sunday. I hope you sensed something of the presence of God's Spirit as we worshiped and that you felt genuinely welcomed by people in the congregation. I'm glad that you took the opportunity to talk with people at the fellowship meal, + were able to remain afterward for the congregational meeting. The combination of activities probably gave you a good introduction to our church.

I'm sending you a one page sheet which tells a bit more about the church—some of our activities and history. I welcome the opportunity to sit down with you and talk further if you'd like. If I can be of service in any way, do not hesitate to phone (777–7777).

Peace,
[David Geist]

ABOUT THE PHILADELPHIA FELLOWSHIP

Philadelphia Mennonite Fellowship began in 1984, growing out of a neighborhood Bible study group of West Philadelphians. Today the group is about 140 people. About 30% of us are from Mennonite background; other church backgrounds are Catholic, Episcopal, Methodist, Presbyterian, Friends, Nazarene, Assemblies of God, Baptist, Christian and Missionary Alliance, and Brethren. We are from the U.S. and from 7 other countries.

The group meets for worship at 10:30 Sunday mornings in the Philadelphia Theological Seminary building at 7777 Chestnut (two doors east of the corner of 43rd and Chestnut).

Sunday School is provided for children and youth during the worship service. Twice each year adult electives are offered prior to the service for an eight week period. Once a month there is a fellowship meal after the service. The Lord's Supper is also observed monthly. Small Bible study and support groups meet in members' homes during the week.

Among [Philadelphia Fellowship's] special projects are a food co-op and a meals delivery program. The latter provides meals for the homebound elderly in the community. Some members cook and package the meals while others deliver them to the homebound and offer friendship.

Another project is a regular International Forum which presents speakers from other countries or Americans who have lived abroad highlighting the political, religious and economic situations in those countries. [Philadelphia Fellowship] has had an international focus since its beginning. Members or former members live and serve in seven different countries: Botswana, Uganda, Egypt, Indonesia, Thailand, Chad, and Vietnam. A pastoral intern from Sri Lanka recently completed a term of service with the Fellowship.

Also, the congregation recently entered a covenant partnership with Habitat for Humanity, a Christian non-profit ministry that rehabilitates houses with and for poor families.

[Philadelphia Fellowship] is one of 14 Mennonite churches in the city. Philadelphia is home to the oldest Mennonite church in North America (Germantown, 1683) and some of the newest. Mennonites in Philadelphia are black, white, and Asian and worship in English, Spanish, Chinese and Vietnamese.

SHORTLY AFTER HE sent me the letter and the one-page sheet, David Geist and I had lunch at my house. I told him then that I hoped to write a book that would be based partly on the experiences I had while visiting his congregation. Geist was, I think, a little amused when he found out about my project: a potential member of the congregation had turned out to be something other. He was not, however, particularly upset to learn what I was up to, and he certainly never did anything to discourage my work. On the contrary, he and the other members of the church always treated me with courtesy. They encouraged me to participate in a wide range of church-related activities. They let me attend their worship services. They invited me to members' houses where small groups of people met to pray and to study the Bible. They let me share their potluck suppers. They let me watch the business meetings in which the church made its corporate decisions.

The people at the fellowship drove me to Washington, D.C., to watch a congressional committee hold hearings on a bill that would have allowed Mennonites—and other conscientious objectors to U.S. military expenditures—to direct their taxes away from the Pentagon and toward activities that were less tainted by violence.[5] They asked me to read certain books, which I found fascinating and provocative. They invited me to sing songs that I liked. They encouraged me to tell them what was going on in my life and then prayed for me. They invited me to share the Lord's Supper with them.[6]

I don't know as much as I would like about what the people at the Philadelphia Mennonite Fellowship made of me. I do know, however, that during the first service I attended, some of my actions—taking notes during the sermon, for instance—were thought (I later found out) to be inappropriate. I know, too, that one person said that when she first saw me she thought I looked either "intense" or "serious" or "depressed" while the service was going on. Later, perhaps because she saw me laugh or heard me make jokes, her impression changed. She said that I seemed easier to talk to than she thought I would be.

My hunch is that the woman to whom I just referred might have seen me as, among many other things, an eligible bachelor. It is possible that two or three other members of the congregation did, too. I also sometimes had the impression that I was seen as a representative of a dominant culture. At one meeting I attended early in my fieldwork, one of the members of the congregation who knew a little about me quickly got on record that I was a professor. Almost immediately thereafter I was quizzed about my degrees. So, although I felt that I fit into the congregation fairly well, and although people who went to services with me sometimes suspected that I might be a member of the fellowship, I never really fit in completely. Again and again, things happened to remind me of that.

For instance, not having a car, I rode a bike to the services. That was fine, that made me fit. But there was something too splashy about my bike. It looked too expensive, and its yellow-green color was too fluorescent. My clothes were not right, either. They shouldn't have come from Lands End and J. Crew. So even when I dressed down—which I almost always did—my clothes cost more than theirs. Even when I read with considerable care the book that was supposed to guide a Bible study group, I did so incorrectly. I pushed its arguments in directions that several other members found odd. My readings would have struck them, I think, as overly academic or as lacking in common sense or as too theoretical or too fancy.

No one at the group ever criticized me for going to an Episcopal church. In fact, the people I met at the Philadelphia Mennonite Fellowship who knew the particular congregation I generally attended had heard good things about it. But my Episcopalianness marked me, I think, as a representative of a dominant culture. They loved the radical reformation; I was associated with the magisterial one. They were spiritual descendants of Menno Simons; I was a descendant of the religious tradition associated with Henry VIII. My people were, in a way, those who had persecuted their people. Their people were martyrs; my people weren't. But this issue never became a bone of contention between us, in part because they were able to think of me not as an Episcopalian but rather as a former Southern Baptist and a "Mennonite camp-follower" (a phrase Geist used to describe how the people in his congregation thought of me).

As far as I could tell, no one in the Philadelphia Mennonite Fellowship thought of me as someone who needed to be saved by accepting Jesus Christ. That made my fieldwork at the fellowship less tricky and less exhausting than at the Philadelphia Church of Christ or at Oak Grove.[7]

In any case, it would be easy to exaggerate the amount of time the people at the Philadelphia Mennonite Fellowship spent thinking about me. Even as my fieldwork was coming to a close, research assistants who were working on the project were running into people there who did not seem to know that I existed. Indeed, to this day I still see people from the fellowship on the street or in a shop without receiving any sign of recognition.

GOVERNING THE CHURCH AND INTERPRETING THE BIBLE

Once, while I was driving to Washington, D.C., to attend a congressional hearing with several of the people from the fellowship, I found myself in the middle of a conversation about whether the Letter to the Ephesians was a Pauline text, a pseudo-Pauline text, or a text made up of Pauline fragments. At the time, it didn't seem unusual to be talking about such matters in the course of traveling to a congressional hearing about what to do with people who wanted to avoid paying taxes to support the U.S. military. But the next day, as I thought over what we had said, the whole conversation did seem a little odd. During my years in Philadelphia, I had probably had a hundred or so conversations about the Phillies for every one about Ephesians or any of the other books in the Bible. In the circles I run in, a well-thought-out position on Ephesians is thought to be characteristic of only two sorts of people: professors who teach the New Testament and religious fanatics.

Of course, not all the people in the Philadelphia Mennonite Fellowship had a well-reasoned position on the authorship of Ephesians. Nearly all of them, however, knew a great deal about the Scriptures. Time and time again in the course of my fieldwork the people at the fellowship surprised me—even intimidated me a little—with how much they knew. It was taken for granted, for example, that a serious Christian would know enough about the Book of Psalms, the Hebrew alphabet, and biblical scholarship to realize that many of the psalms form acrostics. It was also assumed—or at least *almost* assumed—that serious Christians would know how to flip from one scriptural passage to another and then to a third as they were discussing religious matters. These people knew, for example, how to get from the fifth chapter of the Letter of James to the fifth chapter of the Gospel of Matthew to the sixth chapter of Amos in an eyeblink. In the context of the Philadelphia Mennonite Fellowship, possessing such a skill was not worth commenting on. Lacking it was what was odd.

The people devoted a good deal of time, as you might expect, to individual Bible study. In fact, a good many of them incorporated Bible study into their daily routines. But what I found particularly striking was the degree to which their Bible reading was also explicitly and self-consciously communal. They habitually gathered *together* to read the Bible and to talk about out how the Bible should influence their thoughts and actions.

It would be inaccurate to describe these people as fundamentalists. But they did have tendencies that might strike many outsiders, including someone like me, as fundamentalistic. For example, most Christians who attend the sort of religious congregations I am used to are willing to say: "That passage of the Scriptures asserts x; nevertheless y is the case." I'm not sure that I ever heard any of the Mennonites say anything like that. That is, they took what the Scriptures say on every aspect of human life very, very seriously. They believed that God reveals himself to humans largely (though not, of course, exclusively) through the Bible. They firmly believed that Christians ought to let the Bible exercise a great deal of control—mastery even—over their lives.

The people did not put a great deal of emphasis on the passages of Scripture that celebrate the Israelites' conquest of Canaan and the victories of King David's armies. They also deemphasized the passages that celebrate patriarchal practices, prosperity, and the power of the state. And rather than focusing (as do many Protestants) on the letters of Paul and on what those letters say about Christ, the people at the Philadelphia Mennonite Fellowship focused on the synoptic Gospels—Matthew, Mark, and Luke—and on what they say about Jesus and about the kingdom of God.[8]

Such a focus is not, obviously, the only possible reading of the synoptic Gospels, but neither is it a terribly idiosyncratic one. One of the books in my study—published by a Roman Catholic publisher— asserts that "that which gives meaning to Jesus' life, activity, and fate, is the kingdom of God."[9] Another—a reference work by Presbyterians and Anglicans—says that "the centrality of the idea of the kingdom of God . . . in the teaching of Jesus is beyond all question."[10]

Although I did not fully understand precisely how the people interpreted "the kingdom of God," I am almost certain that they believed its nature was revealed in scriptural passages such as the Sermon on the Plain in the sixth chapter of the Gospel of Luke. It suggests that when the kingdom of God comes, the world will be turned upside down. People who are rich and who have enough to eat will find a kingdom of "woe," but people who are hungry and poor will become "blessed." And those who are "reviled" in the present world will also be singled out for God's blessing when the kingdom of God arrives.

Most of the women and men in the Philadelphia Mennonite Fellowship knew that in the history of Christianity, Christians tried to violently overthrow the kingdoms of this world to pave the way for the kingdom of God. Thus, a few of the people expressed a good deal of sympathy, from time to time, with people who were willing to use violence to resist oppression. And several of them encouraged me to read a book that stressed the similarities between Jesus and bandits who used violence against the established powers.[11]

However, it is hard to imagine any of the people actually trying to use violence to usher in the kingdom of God, which they believed is associated with—even defined by—peace. They believed that its coming is signaled by swords being beaten into plowshares and spears into pruning hooks. The people in the fellowship viewed the use of violence to prepare the way for God's kingdom as almost blasphemous. To them, it seemed clear that Christians who longed for its arrival ought to lay aside their swords and spears and pray that God would transform them into "children" and "servants" of "God's peace."[12]

Trying to live their lives without relying on violence forced the Mennonites to confront a number of difficult questions. What should I do when I am on a subway car and a man sitting next to me begins to behave in ways that suggest he might be a threat to my safety? Do I have any choice other than to allow my son to be beaten up by the bullies at his school? Is it appropriate for me to rely on the police for protection from violent criminals? Should I take a self-defense course to try to keep from being raped? Should I refuse to pay war taxes?[13]

These sorts of questions came up fairly regularly in the worship services and Bible studies sponsored by the fellowship. The people rarely claimed that Christian Scripture gave them clear-cut guidance, although it did make clear that the peaceable kingdom had—in some unspecified but important sense—already begun to break into human history. They believed that it *was* possible for Christians—even Christians living in Philadelphia in the early 1990s—to learn how to live their lives without relying on violence.[14]

The framework of the worship services was provided in part by a hymnal that contained a sweeping affirmation of faith, which included the following:

> Jesus taught us to speak of hope as the coming of God's kingdom. We believe that God is at work in our world turning hopeless and evil situations into good. We believe that goodness and justice will triumph in the end and that tyranny and oppression cannot last forever. One day all tears will be wiped away; the lamb will lie down with the lion, and justice will roll down like a mighty stream. True peace and true reconciliation are not only desired, they are assured and guaranteed in Christ. This is our hope. This is our faith.[15]

Thus, the people were confident that the peaceable kingdom is eventually going to triumph over violent ones. However, they did not fool themselves into believing that they were living in a world in which the kingdom of God was fully manifest. The ways in which it was not were discussed with some frequency and with a good deal of passion in the worship services sponsored by the fellowship.

During a service, for instance, that took place shortly after a national event that many members of the fellowship found particularly appalling, a woman said: "I feel like I do not have any recourse." The American state, she said, always seems to find ways to buy weapons and to support the military, but the state treats its cities and the people who live in them with a "criminal" neglect.[16] A man made a similar observation: "I have a lot of anger," he said, "about the directions our country is going in." More and more of the nation's wealth is controlled by the very richest of its citizens. The state is not spending money in a way that gives all its citizens decent educations. It is spending lots of money on locking people up in prisons. The state seems to devote more of its energy to executing people than it has in the recent past. "We need," the man said, "to spend some time in prayer."

The Mennonites did not assume that everyone who spent a lot of time praying for the coming of the kingdom of God would necessarily live a life full of suffering. However, they did believe that everyone who did so opened themselves up to trouble. They believed that the empires of Jesus' day did not worry much about taking actions that resulted in their subjects' suffering. They didn't think that twentieth-century empires particularly cared how much suffering and death they caused, either.

The people in the fellowship certainly did not believe that a person who prayed for the kingdom of God should assume that she or he would live a long and happy life. The man who preached the Sermon on the Plain didn't get to live such a life, nor did all the saints of the first and sixteenth centuries. Indeed at least one of the Mennonites' texts suggested that a person who longed for the kingdom of God should expect this life to be full of failure and disappointment.[17]

In part, perhaps because they focused so much of their attention on God's kingdom, the people were not at all reluctant to speak of God as a "monarch" or to celebrate his "lordship." But their emphasis on God's lordship did not produce a commitment to the support of lordship and hierarchy in the church or in other human communities. The fact that God is lord of all ought to lead Christians to scrutinize all human claims to authority with great care. People who are rich, well educated, connected to the state, in control of weapons, white, and ordained are used to assuming their right to lordship, but such assumptions, the people believed, are challenged by the fact that God is lord of all.

Although the people in the Philadelphia Mennonite Fellowship acknowledged that human hierarchies can often exercise a powerful influence over human imaginations, they also asserted that such hierarchies are not what they pretend to be: inevitable and God-ordained. Christians do not have to treat such hierarchies as natural. With God's help, they can learn to treat them with indifference, thus allowing themselves to experiencing the presence of God in their day-to-day lives.

So it is not surprising that when my friend Bruce Comens visited the Philadelphia Mennonite Fellowship, he was especially struck by the way in which the worship services celebrated and embodied egalitarianism. "This church offered," he concluded, "about the most egalitarian sense of social politics I could imagine in such an organization. Repeatedly, and as a necessary part of the service—I mean, it was never strained or some kind of superficial demonstration—all members of the congregation were involved in the service as more or less equal members."[18] Indeed, what Comens saw and heard at the church led him to suspect that the congregation's commitment to democracy was stronger than its commitment to doctrine or mission. "The church was," he concluded, "based around specific ideas of community—of democracy, etc.—rather than, say, a theological doctrine or an evangelical mission."[19] I am not sure that I agree with Comens's conclusion. I talked to many members of the church who clearly cared a great deal about "theology" and "missions." But Comens was surely right to emphasize the congregation's hostility to human hierarchy. The fact that its members believed that their congregation ought not to "go in for hierarchy" was one of the the defining characteristics of the Philadelphia Mennonite Fellowship.[20]

Of course, the fellowship was not, in fact, free from all traces of hierarchy. It seemed clear that on some of the issues, Geist had more influence than any other single member of the congregation. Geist had, as I have already suggested, a good deal of erudition. The members of the fellowship had a lot of respect for learning. Geist's views were, accordingly, treated with much respect.

His views were not, however, held in awe. In the course of my fieldwork it became clear to me that the services at the Philadelphia Mennonite Fellowship were routinely arranged so that the congregation could comment on Geist's sermon after it was preached. During these discussion times, the people who had heard the sermon seemed perfectly willing to express views that ran directly counter to those that he had set forth.

Also no one at the fellowship would have dreamed of calling David Geist "Father." The church thought of itself as a "sisterhood" and a "brotherhood."[21] Everyone there, including Geist, was seen as a child of God. No one was seen as God's special representative to the other members of the congregation,[22] and they certainly did not think Geist was "in charge" of the church. They tended to treat any suggestion that he might be with some impatience. "Isn't," they asked, "God in charge of the church?"[23] Geist was at most a part of "a team of elders."[24]

The congregation made its decisions about how its affairs should be run in a way that avoided giving Geist or the other elders of the church too much authority. Most of those decisions were made in business meetings, which greatly emphasized "consensus" and "democracy" and which were self-consciously designed to deemphasize human hierarchies. All the people who attended services at the Philadelphia Mennonite Fellowship—members and nonmembers alike—were encouraged to participate in these meetings. And although nonmembers did not have full voting rights in the business meetings, the meetings *were* structured in such a way as to give them a fair amount of say in the deliberations. The meetings certainly were not run in a way that encouraged laypeople to defer to the views of those who were ordained. In fact, the person who ran the meetings was not Geist but a layperson.[25]

CAESAR

When I began my fieldwork at the Philadelphia Mennonite Fellowship, I thought that the congregation would have a hard time separating itself from the assumptions of the secular, American political left. I thought it likely, for instance, that the people would not distinguish too sharply between the traditions of the Christian faith and those of the left wing of the Democratic party. I thought they might think about politics in a way that was similar to—perhaps even simply a mirror image of—the way people in the new Christian right think about politics. This proved not to be the case.

At one point in the worship service on January 12, 1992, Geist noted that Philadelphia's new mayor, Ed Rendell, had been inaugurated just a few days earlier, and he then prayed that the new leaders of the city (presumably the people in the Rendell administration) would treat the city's inhabitants compassionately. But I cannot recall anything else being said during the worship service or the business meeting that directly concerned partisan politics. Moreover, nothing suggested that the people believed that becoming deeply involved in partisan politics was the key to living a life with as much integrity as the lives of the saints who lived in the first and sixteenth centuries.

Actually, *a marked lack of interest* in partisan politics turned out to be a defining characteristic of the worship services I attended at the Philadelphia Mennonite Fellowship. The service two days before the November 1992 elections, for example, did not include any systematic discussion about the upcoming election. Nor did it include any indication that the fellowship was part of a "get out the vote" campaign.

Though the worship service that had been held the week before did include a sermon that discussed partisan politics, its analysis was fairly bleak. It warned that Christians ought not to get too involved in partisan politics; it suggested that the "primary [political] duty" of Christians is to "pray for justice," partly because doing so could help them prevent their view of the world from being unduly influenced by the norms of the American political system.[26]

One day before I started my fieldwork, I was at St. Mary's Episcopal Church on Bainbridge Street with a group of people who were trying to make the place look a little less run down. While we were cleaning, I asked the vicar of the church if she would mind if I put the U.S. flag in an attic, where it would be out of sight. The vicar, a Latina whose view of the world had been shaped by liberation theology, said she thought that was a good idea, and so the flag disappeared. Later—after my fieldwork was over—that vicar left St. Mary's, and the man who replaced her did not share her views. The flag was again placed near the altar.

Not many of the people in the Philadelphia Mennonite Fellowship would find it easy to sit through a worship service in a room where the American flag was so prominently displayed. In fact, many of them would have found such a display deeply disturbing. During a talk he gave to one of my classes at Temple, Geist was asked why there was no flag in his congregation's sanctuary. He responded by making an allusion to Antiochus's desecration of the temple in Jerusalem. "The American flag," he said, "is the abomination of desolation." The remark was meant as a joke, but just barely. He really did think that putting the U.S. flag in a Christian sanctuary was an abomination and that it actually was somewhat comparable to sacrificing a pig in a temple dedicated to worshiping Yahweh.

Geist and the other members of the fellowship did not want the worship services sponsored by their congregation to legitimize chauvinism or to give any indication that they believed the American state was holy. They wanted the services instead to provide a forum for questioning and contesting the logic of nation-states. They wanted the tension between nation-states and the kingdom of God to be emphasized rather than played down.

In 1992, the Philadelphia Mennonite Fellowship celebrated the first Sunday after the Fourth of July as "Peace Sunday." Fairly early in the service, those of us who were participating recited a litany from *Hymnal: A Worship Book*. The litany seemed to go out of its way to emphasize the tensions between U.S. society and the kingdom of God. It made a point of subordinating the earthly dominions—such as the Republic whose founding is memorialized on the fourth—to the authority of Yahweh:

O God, Sovereign of the universe, without you nothing is true, nothing is just. In your Word you reveal the way of love. By your spirit you make it possible.

From greed and selfishness, from a society in which the rich get richer and the poor get poorer, compassionate God, deliver us.

From racial prejudice and religious intolerance, from a society which makes its weakest and most recent members into scapegoats, compassionate God, deliver us.

From indifference to the needs of other countries, from the delusion that you love any other nation less than you love us, compassionate God, deliver us.

From self-indulgence and indifference, from a society in which fidelity and responsibility have little place, compassionate God, deliver us.

Author of life, give us hearts set on the coming of your reign; give us wise, just, and humble leaders; give all who live in this land a will to live in peace, through Jesus Christ, the One who is above all powers and dominions. Amen.[27]

The worship service that was held on July 4, 1993, also emphasized the tensions between nation-states and the Mennonite's understanding of the kingdom of God.[28] Much of that service was given over to a sermon that criticized the pretensions of the American state in remarkably strong terms. Geist commented on "how hard it has become to distinguish between Christianity and patriotism" and on the various ways in which the flag and the cross have been conflated in the history of Christendom.

Geist was sure that such a conjoining of the symbols of the Christian faith and of the state was entirely inappropriate. He reminded his fellow congregants that Jesus had been put to death on a cross because he did and said things that did not accord with the wishes of the Roman Empire. Geist did not see how modern followers of Jesus could legitimately expect to establish warm and friendly relations with the people who ran the empires under whose reign they lived.[29]

In analyzing the nature of the American empire, Geist went so far as to compare it to the "beast" that figures so prominently in the Revelation to John. In Geist's sermon, the beast was not what it so often has been in the sermons preached by Bible-carrying Christians in the United States—a symbol for that which imperils the American Republic or the American way of life. It was, rather, a way of describing what the American state was like.

The Mennonites did not produce a coherent analysis of the American state. Their analyses were, rather, atheoretical and ad hoc; they focused primarily on two particular points at which the working of the state seemed to them to impinge on Christians' efforts to live a godly life. The first point concerned sovereignty: the people believed that recognizing and celebrating God's sovereignty over the world of nature and the affairs of human beings was an integral part of living a godly life and that the American state claimed a sovereignty for itself that contested the authority of God. The state, as they saw it, tended to act as though it and not God was sovereign over the people within its borders. It demanded from them a sort of allegiance that was greater than that which could be reconciled with life lived with a full awareness of the sovereignty of God.

The people knew, of course, that the men and women who ran the state are often quite willing to admit that there is some sense in which the state's sovereignty is subordinate to that of God. But the people also believed that that admission was usually somewhat perfunctory. The sovereignty of God was given lip service, but in practice it was ignored, reduced to a mere abstraction. The state wanted the people to live in a way that made it clear that as a practical matter their allegiance to the state was more important to them than their allegiance to the ruler of the universe. It required the people to treat the demands it made on them as though they were more pressing and fundamental than the demands made by God. Although the state was willing to tolerate a Christian who said, "My ultimate allegiance is not to the state," in fact, Christians who actually lived their lives in accord with the sovereignty of God were seen as untrustworthy and subversive.[30]

The second point concerned violence. The people believed that a godly life was by definition a peaceable life. They also believed that the

American state was founded on and maintained by the use of violence and that it wanted all the people to give their support, either directly or indirectly, to its violent actions. The state pushed Americans to produce weapons for its use, to volunteer to kill and die to help it achieve its aims, to celebrate those occasions when it had used force of arms to humiliate its foes, and to provide it with money to pay a vast network of violence-making men and machines.

The Mennonites were encouraged to believe that Christians had a duty to minimize the support they gave to this violent network. The people were taught that they should not serve in the armed forces or work in weapons production for the armed forces. They were encouraged to help organize demonstrations against wars fought by the U.S. government and to consider the possibility that they might want to become war-tax resisters. At least two of the people in the fellowship had refused to pay the portion of their taxes that supported the American military, and at least one of them had gotten into a lot of trouble with the U.S. government.

That sort of concrete resistance to the claims the state makes on the people who live under its jurisdiction was accompanied by a less dramatic but equally important form of resistance that focused on ceremony and ritual. The fellowship encouraged the people to devote a good deal of their lives to participating in rituals that celebrated the sovereignty of God *and* to devote relatively little time to ceremonies—such as saluting the American flag or singing the "Star-Spangled Banner"—that celebrated the sovereignty of the state. People were encouraged to view any intermingling of the two sorts of rituals with great suspicion.

It would probably be a mistake to dismiss this pattern of behavior as a merely symbolic variety of resistance to the claims of modern nation-states. It is "symbolic," of course, but probably not "merely." By carefully picking and choosing their rituals, the people routinely reminded themselves who they were and where their ultimate loyalties ought to lie.

However, nearly all the Mennonites paid war taxes. Their doing so was in many respects simply a matter of staying true to the traditions of their forebears. Mennonites in North America have only rarely tried to avoid paying those portions of their taxes they know will be used to support state-directed violence, although there is a long tradition of trying to maintain distance between themselves and the state in which they live.[31] Given this tradition, it is perhaps surprising how little pressure the fellowship brought to bear on its members to isolate themselves and their households from the claims of the state. The fellowship did not ask its members to give up professions, such as the law, that necessarily enmeshed them pretty deeply in workings of the state. Nor did it discourage its members from serving as jurors in criminal cases or from casting votes in electoral contests in which the winner would have to be willing to use violence to fulfill the duties of office.

Although most of the people associated with the fellowship were ideologically predisposed toward quite skeptical analyses of the state, one certainly did not have to publicly denounce it to become a member of the Philadelphia Mennonite Fellowship. In reality, many of the congregation believed that it was a mistake to assert, as David Geist did, that the state was essentially un-Christian. They thought that such an assertion rested on an interpretation of the state that was extreme and unbalanced. American society in general and the state in particular were less un-Christian than people like Geist made them out to be.[32] Some of the people believed, for instance, that it was a mistake to interpret the state *primarily* as a set of institutions that were maintained by and devoted to the use of violence. Although they admitted that such an interpretation was strongly rooted in Mennonite tradition, these members asserted that it did not accord well with their own experience, which had convinced them that the state sometimes tamed and controlled violence.

A particularly articulate member of the congregation—a lawyer—asserted, for instance, that the criminal justice systems maintained by the state sometimes produced such results. That is, sometimes they really did help people who had committed violent crimes to straighten out their lives; sometimes they did reform people who had committed violent crimes. Such positive outcomes had to be taken seriously if Christians were going to reach an accurate understanding of the state.[33]

This sort of somewhat grudging admiration did not, of course, amount to a claim that the American state was in some strong sense "Christian." The claim was far milder than that, something akin to saying that "the American state sometimes takes actions which lead to results that a Christian is likely to find heartening." Still, even a grudging admission that state-supported coercion sometimes had beneficial effects undercut the sharp distinction people like Geist tried to maintain between the actions of the state and those human activities that were congruent with living in expectation of the kingdom of God. And, in truth, that distinction was by no means evident to all the members of the fellowship. Eleanor Gregory, for instance, was familiar with and attracted to those strands within the traditions of U.S. Protestantism that tended to interpret the state, at least at the time of its founding, as a "godly"—even as a "Christian"—organization. Although Gregory did not think that the state, as it presently existed, was a fully Christian organization, neither did she assume that "a Christian state" was a contradiction in terms. In fact, there might well have been a side to her that longed for a return to a time when Christians living in the United States could think of the American government as a Christian institution rather than as a secular one.[34]

MAMMON

The Mennonites viewed rituals associated with America's entertainment industries—such as going to a theater to see a Hollywood movie or to an auditorium to hear a rock concert—somewhat less warily than they did rituals that buttressed the authority of nation-states. The people, however, were sure that Christians ought to minimize the amount of time they spent ingesting commercial entertainment. For example, it was a mistake for Christians to spend much time watching commercial television, which they regarded simply as a tool that manufacturers used to "promote their products." The little "entertainments" that were interspersed between the commercials were, they thought, merely decorative.[35]

In general, the Mennonites did not believe that followers of Jesus were likely to accumulate enough money to buy very many of the products promoted on commercial television. Jesus had, they believed, been "very poor"; often, he must not have known "where his next meal was coming from."[36] Trying to follow him probably would not lead to the sort of life that enabled one to accumulate enough money to worry about making any kind of systematic financial investments.[37] It might well lead to economic poverty.

The Mennonites thought that people who devoted a good deal of their energy to earning enough money to be able to afford two cars, nice furniture, beautiful art, and a house in a nice neighborhood were making a terrible mistake. Such an assignment of energy was worldly and un-Christian.[38] The people were extremely skeptical of attempts to show that following Jesus might lead to economic prosperity. They viewed men who tried to do so—men like Zig Zigler, Robert Schuller, and exponents of "prosperity theology"—with a good deal of hostility.[39]

The Mennonites assumed that living a Christian life involved spending a lot of one's time doing things that are, when judged by the standards of economic rationality, silly. They also believed that it was important for Christians to find time each week to self-consciously refrain from taking part in any activities that are directed toward making money.[40] And whatever money that Christians "earned" during the rest of the week actually belonged to God. People who wanted to live a Christian life had to realize that they were simply stewards of whatever money had come into their hands and that they were therefore obliged to use it to see to the basic material needs of others, as well as of themselves.[41]

The actions of the Mennonites were not, of course, completely consistent with the fellowship's economic ideals. Nevertheless, there did seem to be a good deal of congruence between those ideals and the way in which the members lived their lives. The Mennonites certainly did not focus their energies exclusively on activities that could help them accumulate wealth. Instead, they devoted huge amounts of time to such things as studying the Bible or helping neighbors who had fallen on hard times—actions that many economists would regard as irrational. Few of the people followed career paths that produced great wealth. Some worked for wages only a few hours a week; a few did not work for wages at all. A great many of them had jobs—such as teaching in Christian elementary schools—that were poorly paid. Even those who worked in potentially lucrative fields such as the law seemed to gravitate toward the kind of work (providing legal advice to the poor, for example) that did not pay especially well.

The people generally lacked many of the hallmarks of a high standard of living. Many could not afford to eat in expensive restaurants or to buy fashionable clothes. Although the houses they lived in tended to look "neat" and "tidy," they rarely contained many possessions that were "new" or "valuable."[42] Moreover, they were often located in poor neighborhoods that were riddled with crime.[43]

The people associated with the fellowship seemed to do a fairly good job of insulating themselves and their families from cultural products manufactured by the entertainment industries. Gregory's household, for example, was run in a way that prevented her children from watching very much television. The television they did watch was largely confined to holiday shows, documentaries, and sports. Her children did not see very many Hollywood movies, either. The movies they tended to see were made by Christians and shown in a theater called Cinema 43, which did not charge admission.

However, the children who grew up in these households were not by any means fully insulated from the world of commerce, a world that included many advertisements and much commercial entertainment. Nor were the households fully insulated from the logic of economic rationality. The people did—from time to time at least—make financial investments with an eye toward getting a good rate of return rather than adhering strictly to biblical injunctions concerning usury.[44]

The households also were not fully insulated from the desire to obtain a high standard of living that is so characteristic of people who live in a commercialized culture. Some of the people freely admitted that the desire for a high standard of living played a large role in shaping the way in which their own households and the households of their fellow congregants were run. They did not believe that either their own households or many others associated with the fellowship were free of materialistic excess.[45]

To maintain this (relatively) high standard of living, these households had to have a steady influx of wages. Not all of these wages came from commercial enterprises, but some of them did. And a very large proportion, indeed, came from organizations that were run by people who were terribly interested in the "bottom line" and in the "efficient" delivery of goods and services.[46] These jobs put a lot of pressure on people's households. Workers were forced to spend long hours away from their families most days of the week, and many of them had to spend a lot of the time they were at home recovering from or worrying about strains created by their jobs.[47]

It seems clear, then, that the Mennonites were not fully isolated from the world of commerce. Nor was the Philadelphia Mennonite Fellowship itself an impregnable fortress. When the members talked about the church's affairs, they sometimes did so in language that was more commercial than biblical: they talked about getting monetary grants, about making sure that the necessary finances were in place, about making sound investments, and about being cost effective. And when the church wanted to attract new members, it sometimes relied on techniques—involving demographic surveys and phone solicitations—that were used by business firms to attract new customers.

For the church to meet its budget, it had to rely, in part at least, on contributions from people whose income came, either directly or indirectly, from commercial enterprises. If all the members of the congregation had simultaneously chosen to do whatever it took to separate themselves completely from the world of commercial enterprise, the fellowship might well have had to close its doors. The Philadelphia Mennonite Fellowship's relationship to the world of commerce was not, then, simply adversarial. It was also, to some degree at least, parasitic.

CHRISTIAN FAMILY VALUES

The worship services at the Philadelphia Mennonite Fellowship rarely—in fact, almost never—warned against pouring too much of one's energy into one's own family. Rather, the services generally legitimized, reinforced, and sacralized family bonds. Devoting a huge proportion of one's life to one's family was seen as congruent with living a devout Christian life. It wasn't seen as selfish, worldly, or un-Christian.[48] The people wanted to make their families into places where their sons and daughters came to see Christian standards as natural and the standards of the world as bizarre. They wanted them to be places where their children would realize that they could, and ought to, "have a relationship with the Lord" and where they learned "what a real relationship with Christ look[s] like."[49]

The fellowship's attachment to family life seemed to shape nearly every aspect of its worship services, for example, the way in which the congregation arranged themselves in their seats as they prepared for worship (they tended to clump together as families). It also influenced the sorts of songs that were sung and the stories that were told in the course of worship. Nearly every Sunday, the worship service included stories and songs designed to appeal especially to the children in the congregation.

The fellowship's attachment to families was especially clear during the part of the worship service that was set aside for people to talk about things that were sources of joy or of concern and then to ask for their fellow congregants' prayers.[50] More often than not, what people said during this period concerned their families—a son or daughter who was ill, a spouse who was about to leave for a long bike trip, a sibling who was in Guatemala doing union organizing, or a child who was having difficulty in sleeping through the night. The people in the fellowship took it for granted that God had a deep interest in their families, that family life was a focus of God's concern. He cared more about that than he did about partisan politics.

At the Philadelphia Mennonite Fellowship, God was also pictured as a being who had given humanity a set of commands concerning sexuality that were clear-cut, restrictive, and highly significant. God certainly was not a being who approved of "sexual liberation" as it is constructed in contemporary U.S. culture.[51]

Although a few of the unmarried members of the fellowship were sexually active, sex outside of marriage was generally viewed with a great deal of suspicion. People who were not married and who were sexually active were sometimes asked to step down from leadership positions. They were regarded as poor role models for the children in the congregation. They were seen as failing to adhere to biblical norms.[52]

As the Mennonites understood it, the Bible did not give Christians any reason to think that expressing one's sexual desires just for the sake of doing so was worthwhile. Nor did the Bible suggest that "sexual fulfillment" was one of the hallmarks of a godly life. Rather, the Bible taught that sexual urges that did not focus on one's spouse ought to be suppressed; being a Christian meant that you can't always have what you want.

There were some striking differences between the way that homosexuality was viewed at the Philadelphia Mennonite Fellowship and the way it was viewed at Oak Grove. In the course of my fieldwork at the fellowship, I never heard Geist preach a sermon that endorsed Christian political crusades to prop up "traditional family values" or that condemned homosexuality. Nor did I ever hear him parody or ridicule homosexuals. In fact, in a private conversation, he said that he himself was boycotting a particular business because its hiring practices discriminated against lesbians and gays. Such discrimination was, he seemed to feel, un-Christian.

At least one of the persons I talked to—a woman in her 30s who made her living as a writer—told me that although there had been a time in her life when she was sure that homosexuality was sinful, she had now begun to have some doubts about whether the matter was quite as clearcut as she had once thought.[53] Although most of the people at the Philadelphia Mennonite Fellowship did not seem to share that woman's doubts, neither did they ever say anything to me or to my research assistants that was analogous to the harsh denunciations of homosexuality we encountered at Oak Grove. When, for example, Margaret Drake talked to Dwyer-McNulty (one of my research assistants) about homosexuality, she told her that although the Bible makes it clear that homosexuality is sinful, the Bible also makes it clear that Christians need to steer clear of a spirit of "condemnation." Christians' attitudes toward homosexuals ought to be characterized, Drake said, by a spirit of "love and peace." She also told Dwyer-McNulty that two of the women who lived in her neighborhood were (she guessed) a lesbian couple and that she had a good relationship with them. The couple's attitude to her was friendly, and they were good neighbors. Drake wasn't about to tell them that they were living in sin.

If a person wanted to join a community in Philadelphia where heterosexuality was not seen as normative, there would be better places to look than the Philadelphia Mennonite Fellowship. Actually, there would be better places to look in the same neighborhood. There were a number of organizations in Philadelphia—including a few churches—where homosexuality was viewed with much less suspicion than it was at the fellowship. Some of the members believed that "tolerance for homosexuality" had "very negative" effects on American families.[54] And nearly all the people were sure that "the Bible speaks very clearly about homosexuality"; it tells us that "homosexuality is a sin."[55]

This suspicion of homosexuality was more than a mere "prejudice." It was based in large part on a careful reading of a set of texts the people at the fellowship believed to be sacred. To them, the Bible did not simply naturalize heterosexuality. It came close to sacralizing it.[56]

The men in the fellowship were not the sort of people who were used to giving orders. They assumed that acting as a servant rather than a commander was part of what it meant to be a follower of Jesus. They did not think of themselves as patriarchs whom their daughters and wives ought to obey. Their demeanor was, all in all, remarkably unassuming.

The women did not assume that they had a duty to defer to male authority. Many of them thought of themselves as feminists. Some of them were probably attracted to the fellowship, in part, at least, because it was somewhat less patriarchal than were many other Bible-carrying Christian congregations.

The women did not refrain from speaking during the congregation's business meetings or worship services. Although they knew that there were passages in the Pauline Epistles indicating that women should not speak in Christian churches, the women believed that these passages did not apply to contemporary Christian communities. They believed that Paul was not setting forth a God-given proscription. He was, rather, simply being "cultural," that is, merely reflecting the biases of the culture in which he had been raised.[57] Although the men often seemed to do more than their share of speaking in the fellowship's public gatherings, speech was sometimes split fairly evenly between the sexes. On occasion, women talked more than men did.[58]

The women were not barred from preaching sermons or from presiding at the Lord's Supper. Nor were they prohibited from serving on any of the church's boards or committees. In fact, the formal rules that governed the fellowship included provisions aimed at making sure that important committees and boards were not made up exclusively of men.[59]

The masculinist elements in the Christian Scriptures were rarely subjected to analysis—much less to systematic critique—at the Philadelphia Mennonite Fellowship. Sometimes (as I have already suggested) they were minimized as being merely "cultural" and as therefore extraneous to the "essential" message of the Bible. More often, they were simply ignored, and thereby allowed to stand without comment and without challenge.

Even a matter as basic as whether or not Bible-carrying Christians ought to picture God as a celestial patriarch did not seem to receive much systematic attention at the fellowship. In general, however, the people did not think that there was anything odd about consistently talking as though God were such a patriarch. Nor did they seem much interested in trying to find ways of thinking about God as a she instead of a he or as a mother rather than as a father.

Although the Mennonites viewed most human hierarchies with a good deal of skepticism, they did not seem to be completely convinced that Christians ought to try hard to put an end to asymmetrical power relationships between women and men. In fact, some of them believed that it would be a mistake to strive to make relationships between men and women "equal" because women are "complements" to men and their relationships to men ideally ought to be "complementary." Trying to make relationships between men and women equal was impractical and unwise.[60]

In part, perhaps, because they both viewed questions connected to gender in such a manner—that is, one that did not assume that equality was a good thing—neither Gregory nor Drake seemed much interested in trying to make their households free of all traces of "patriarchy" or "sexism."[61] The gender roles in both households were fixed and conventional. In both, it was assumed that a husband is the head of all godly families and that a wife will cheerfully submit to her husband's authority.[62]

Neither Gregory nor Drake was particularly interested in ending discrimination against women in the workplace or in giving women more opportunities to pursue careers outside of the home. Gregory thought that the idea that women had to be given "equal pay for equal work" was ill conceived. One's salary ought to be based on what one needed rather than on what one wanted or deserved. Working women who were married to men who made good salaries did not really need high salaries. Their wages therefore, ought, to be fairly low.

Drake believed that women's increasing tendency to pursue careers had been bad for American families; it had led to baby-sitters, day-care workers, and teachers having too much responsibility for shaping the way children in the United States viewed the world. Drake believed, moreover, that women who worked outside of the home sometimes put themselves in situations where it was hard for them to make a real difference in other people's lives. Women who moved into the world of paid work discovered (at least sometimes) that that world was, in the final analysis, confining. Women who stayed at home rather than going out into the world of paid work could, on the other hand, make enormous contributions to the world. They could keep their communities from being neglected. They could "make a mark" on their children.[63]

SIX

THE PHILADELPHIA CHURCH OF CHRIST

REVOLUTION THROUGH RESTORATION

I decided to do fieldwork at the Philadelphia Mennonite Fellowship because I wanted to learn more about a particular variety of Bible-carrying Christianity: a kind that might be described as "radical," "left wing," or "self-consciously alternative." From the very beginning, I thought of the fellowship as a type of Bible-carrying Christianity that I already knew something about.

That was not the case at the Philadelphia Church of Christ. To be sure, it eventually became clear to me that the church had much in common with other congregations that have gotten a good deal of journalistic and scholarly attention in recent years. It insisted on the importance of church growth, on its members' submitting to the authority of their spiritual elders, and on training church leaders in a way that kept them free from the influence of seminaries. Insisting on those three things is something that a number of prominent Bible-carrying Christian congregations have done in recent decades, and so the Philadelphia Church of Christ was hardly sui generis. Indeed, one could well argue that it exemplifies a variety of Bible-carrying Christianity that is already quite large and moderately important and that is very likely to become larger and more important in the next few decades.[1]

But I certainly did not make contact with the Philadelphia Church of Christ because I was looking for a congregation that exemplified a variety of Bible-carrying Christianity that I wanted to learn more about. That the Philadelphia Church of Christ ended up doing that was simply a happy accident.

Indeed I cannot, strictly speaking, even claim that I was the person who initiated my relationship with this church. Things actually started out the other way around. I did not contact the Philadelphia Church of

Christ. Instead, the church contacted me. Two of the church's members invited me to its services; they thought that I would enjoy learning more about their church and about what it stood for.

The first person to tell me about the Philadelphia Church of Christ was a black woman named Angel Jackson. Probably about 18 when I met her, she was one of the students in the honors section of a course in the sociology of religion that I taught in the fall of 1990. She asked me after the course was over if I would like to visit her church. I took the invitation as a compliment of sorts, hearing it as something like this: "I do not know whether you are Christian or not. But you do not seem to have contempt for religion. Maybe you might be interested."

The second person to tell me about the church was another black woman, Candace Hunter. (About 45 when I met her, she had a daughter who was almost the same age as Angel Jackson.) She and I met through an employment agency that provided temporary workers for business offices. I called the service in June 1991 because I wanted to hire someone to proofread a manuscript. Hunter had a great deal of experience as a proofreader and as an editor: she had spent several years working for a university press and was of enormous help to me. It seemed to me that she had memorized the *Chicago Manual of Style*.

In part because the book we were proofreading dealt with the cultural history of U.S. Protestants, Hunter told me something about her religious practices and beliefs while we were proofreading. It turned out that she, like Jackson, was a member of the Philadelphia Church of Christ. She, like Jackson, made a point of asking me to visit her church, partly, I think, because she thought of me as someone whom the church could help; she believed that if I became a member, my life would get better. She also knew, however, that I was looking for a church that I could attend as a way of thinking about Protestants and social power.

I never obtained a text about the Philadelphia Church of Christ that could be compared to the one I was given on the Philadelphia Mennonite Fellowship, partly because the members of the former were not too interested in the Church of Christ qua the Church of Christ. They were far more interested in the church as an outpost of a larger movement, one that was sometimes referred to as International Churches of Christ (Boston Movement).[2]

Walter Elliot, one of the leaders of the church, gave me a history of that movement. "Revolution Through Restoration: From Jerusalem to Rome: From Boston to Moscow" was written by Kip McKean, the movement's founder. It would be difficult to exaggerate the respect accorded to McKean by the other leaders of the movement. Andrew Giambarba, for example, believed that McKean had given spiritual sight to more human beings than had any man or woman who lived in the 1,900 or so years since Apostle Paul preached the gospel.[3]

"Revolution Through Restoration," a photocopy of a typescript, was later published in a magazine called *UpsideDown*.[4] The printed version is the one that I rely on here. McKean includes an admission that some of the stances he first took on issues confronting the movement were mistaken. He notes, for example, that it was wrong to claim that "church leaders could call people to obey and follow them in all areas of opinion." That admission, however, is accompanied by an insistence that "Christians are to obey their leaders in the work of the church." The Bible, McKean asserts, makes that abundantly clear.

McKean repeatedly stresses the incredible success of the movement. It has, for example, helped its members discover the "biblical principles" that govern "godly marriages." Not one of the couples who has "remained faithful to God and his church" has ever gotten a divorce. The movement has also, as he points out in considerable detail, attracted the loyalty of "outstanding men" whose excellent performance in college, in graduate school, and in secular jobs cannot be gainsaid. Alumni of some of the most prestigious educational institutions in the world are devoted members of the movement.

In "Revolution Through Restoration," McKean also details how rapidly the International Churches of Christ (Boston Movement) has grown. Although its roots might be argued to stretch as far back as 1972, one could also say that the movement began on June 1, 1979, in a suburb of Boston with a group of thirty "would-be disciples." Between 1979 and 1991, membership grew from 30 to 37,895. During that time, the number of movement congregations grew from 1 to 103.

McKean does not stress the sociological causes of the movement's growth, which he sees as simply the result of being "God's movement," or of the group's single-minded determination to understand and follow the principles that are set forth in the Bible. However, the growth is linked to several sound decisions that the leaders of the movement have made. They decided, for example, to deemphasize congregational autonomy and instead to build up national and international networks of disciples.

They also decided to place great emphasis on "discipleship partners," a decision that McKean particularly highlights. These partnerships matched "younger, weaker Christians" with "older, stronger" ones. Discipleship partnerships were always same-sex unions. Thus men were never put in a position of being disciples to women, which would be unbiblical. And same-sex unions did not expose people to the "possible temptations" that would have been inherent in partnerships in which women were disciples to men.

The partners were supposed to meet face to face at least once a week. They were also supposed to have "daily contact" with each other. Senior partners could and did give junior partners advice about every aspect of their lives, and junior partners were supposed to take that advice to heart. It was through such advice that "younger, weaker" Christians learned God's will for their lives.

I began fieldwork at the Philadelphia Church of Christ on October 9, 1991, by attending a Wednesday night meeting sponsored by the church. Candace Hunter invited me to the meeting, as I recall, for a particular reason. She knew that I was interested in the relationship between churches and money. She thought it might make sense for me to begin my fieldwork at a meeting at which a lot of attention was directed to that topic.

The meeting was held in an auditorium that had been rented from a private school in one of the wealthy western suburbs of Philadelphia. The school was next to Haverford College.

In 1991, I didn't own a car; it would have been a little difficult for me to get to the church meeting on my own. So Candace and two of her friends—Carlos and Cassandra Wallace—gave me a ride to church. It took us about twenty minutes to drive to Haverford. There, we had coffee at a restaurant near the school where the church met. The block in which the restaurant was located was remarkably prosperous.

We arrived at the meeting about ten minutes before the service itself began. That gave me time to scan the crowd and to talk to people.

The congregation struck me as unusually large. Some of the congregations I have attended almost never get more than 75 or so people on Sunday morning. There were over 200 at this meeting, on a Wednesday night.

The congregants were young. Only about twenty of the people at the meeting were clearly older than I was. I guessed that about 40 percent of the congregation was white and 60 percent was female.[5] Children under 12 went to their own class. I am not sure how many children were present—perhaps twenty or thirty.

One thing that struck me about the service was its relative lack of attention to Bible study. As a child and adolescent, I attended many Wednesday night prayer meetings, which included a lot of time for prayer. But they also included rather more time for studying the Scriptures. Sometimes we would spend half an hour or so talking about—even debating, in a muted sort of way—the precise meaning of a particular verse of Romans or Jeremiah. Before I began my fieldwork I assumed that something like that went on at midweek services of the Philadelphia Church of Christ.

At this particular service, it did not. To be sure, our attention was directed from time to time to passages of Scripture: Malachi 3, Mark 10, Second Corinthians 9, and Philippians 4. But not a single verse of Scripture was read aloud that night, and the talks did not attempt to discern the meaning of particular passages. At one point, we were asked to turn to Malachi 3, but we never got around to reading it. Instead, we just sat there with our Bibles open to the correct page while a man talked for twenty minutes or so about matters that seemed to me—though I may have missed something—to have only the vaguest connection to that chapter.

The service itself started at 7:00 and ended about 9:30. It seemed to me that the main point of the meeting was an announcement. The leaders of the church had decided to raise the church's weekly budget to $8,000, and it was important that the congregation adjust its contributions to the church accordingly.[6]

Given that the budget presentation was the focus of the meeting, and that the congregation was indeed presented with a pamphlet that discussed how much money the church took in and spent each week, you might suspect that the meeting was somewhat boring. It was not, though; it was lively, and there was nothing somber about it. There were many jokes, some of them good enough to make me laugh out loud. The church's increasing financial needs were presented as a good sign—a sign of its spiritual health. Increased need was linked to the fact that "God's kingdom is constantly advancing." This was why the church was "dynamic."

The meeting started with a series of songs. There was no piano, nor any musical instruments at all. I knew a lot of the songs from my days as a Baptist, and they were sung just this side of an outright shout. While we were singing, I almost could imagine being a Bible-carrying Christian again. People applauded after each song, and as the church's various song leaders rotated, people would applaud for their favorites. The song leaders wore slacks, sports coats, and ties. They looked young, successful, and stylish.

From almost the very beginning of the service, I felt as if I were on the set of a TV show. I was struck by the upbeat tone of the meeting and by how often the men who ran it used the word "awesome." It felt a little like a pep rally. People on the stage complimented one another on how well they had performed: for example, "Joe, that was awesome." The slide show with which the meeting concluded—a very professional show, complete with a soundtrack and a good deal of sly humor—was received with much applause and with a lot of laughter.

In part, perhaps, because those of us who were not sitting on the stage were treated as though we were the audience, there was a relatively constricted range of activities in which we could engage. We sang, we applauded, and we said "Amen." That was about the extent of what we were allowed to do. We certainly were not invited to discuss or criticize the new budget. As a matter of fact, we were not even asked to give it a pro forma vote of approval. At one point in the meeting I wondered: "Do we [meaning those of us in the audience] get to vote on the budget?" However, the service was structured to make such a question seem bizarre.

The people who went on the stage to perform were not representative of the congregation as a whole. Both people who gave extended "talks" during the course of the meeting were white men, probably in their late 30s or early 40s. There were four song leaders. One of them (Carlos Wallace) was black; the other three were white. All the song leaders were, I guessed, between the ages of 25 and 35. None of them was a woman. I made a note at some point in the meeting about the way in which gender roles shaped the congregation's public worship: "My impression is that women cannot lead songs nor speak in mixed assemblies."[7] I made a note at some other point about how race figured in the formal theology of the congregation—something such as "Race does not matter."

The two men who gave extended talks made it very clear that money did matter. It mattered a lot. Money had been abused in many religious organizations, bringing shame on Christian people. (The speaker might have had the scandals associated with Jim and Tammy Bakker in mind.) Moreover, some individual Christians sometimes gave so much of their money to the church that they could not meet their other obligations. They did not pay their taxes or their creditors on time. That was irresponsible. One of the speakers said that he had made that sort of mistake when he was young: "I gave too much. I was a little irresponsible."

But though such "irresponsibility" was presented as unwise, a willingness to make individual financial sacrifices was praised. In Old Testament times, one of the speakers said, God told his people to give him 10 percent. What he tells them now, that speaker said, is "I want as much as you can possibly give." God calls us to give more money to his church than seems reasonable by human standards. But the bottom line is not what seems reasonable in the eyes of the world: "The bottom line [a phrase used nearly a dozen times during the service] is faith."

As you can see, being around the Philadelphia Church of Christ sometimes brought out my judgmental side. My fieldnotes brim with negative assessments. In February 1992, after a long conversation with one of the leaders of the church, I claimed that "the form of Christianity [this man] embodied was anti-intellectual, obscurantist, [and] authoritarian." In May 1992, after listening to a talk at the church, I described it as "incoherent." The next month, after attending a worship service, I wrote: "I did not particularly like these people this time."

On the other hand, there were many times in the course of my fieldwork when I acted as a sort of cheerleader for some of the people with whom I had become acquainted. When Carlos Wallace did a good job of leading the congregational singing, I felt relieved and happy. When Walter Elliot preached a sermon the congregation found spellbinding, I felt proud.

There were also a number of times when the church compared favorably with the Southern Baptist churches I had attended between 1957 and 1973. People with degrees from Harvard Divinity School came to the Church of Christ to give talks. No one like that would ever have given a talk at my Southern Baptist churches. At worship services sponsored by the Church of Christ, black men were on the podium, leading the singing and giving talks nearly every Sunday. I don't recall a black man ever leading the singing or giving a talk or delivering a sermon at any of the Southern Baptist churches that I had attended. So sometimes it seemed that the Church of Christ was just superior in some respects to the congregations in which I grew up.

Also, the people in the church were some of the friendliest I have ever met. They responded to my invitations to go places with great avidity. They went to Phillies games and out to dinner with me and came to my house for lunch. They met me at coffeehouses near the University of Pennsylvania and at Temple University. They came to Temple to speak to my classes about their church's doctrines and practices. They were, moreover, always inviting me to do things with them. They asked me to their houses for dinner and to the gym to play basketball. They suggested a day trip to the country to play a simulated war game called Paintball. And they requested—over and over again—that we study the Bible together "one on one."

Much of the attention I received came from the leaders of the church. In fact, some of it came from the leaders of the international movement with which the Philadelphia Church of Christ was associated. Pat Guthrie, who had played a decisive role in shaping the history of that movement, asked me to study the Scriptures with her. She also suggested that I sit next to her at worship services. And when Kip McKean came to the church to speak, he made a point of waving at me and giving me a big smile while he was sitting on the podium. He also made a point of talking to me at some length while we were both playing basketball. McKean seemed to go out of his way to try to make me feel welcome at the church.

In part, perhaps, because they so routinely went out their way to be kind to me, the people at the Philadelphia Church of Christ were perfectly willing to ask for my help in deflecting "attacks" from the outside world. They once asked me, for example, to do whatever I could to get them out of some trouble they had gotten into with Temple University's dean of students.[8] On another occasion they asked me to talk to a TV reporter who was preparing a news report on their church. They were afraid that the report would try to show that the church was "a dangerous religious cult," and they hoped I might prevent that from happening.[9]

These sorts of overt requests were accompanied by a whole set of unspoken requests that I change the way I act, to which, in general, I acceded. For example, I tried to incorporate a set of complicated hand claps into my renditions of Christian hymns. Not doing so would have made me stand out.[10] I also avoided drinking alcoholic beverages while I was with people from the church, and I tried, with some success, to avoid using vulgar language around them.[11] I also tried, with less success, to avoid using "professorial" language,[12] and I did not act or talk with quite so much formality as I was used to.[13] Instead, I tried to be unusually "down-to-earth."

MIGHT AND CONQUEST

Partly by accident and partly by design, I spent Holy Saturday (that is, the day after Good Friday) and Easter Sunday in 1992 in congregations associated with what people often call the Protestant mainstream.

On Holy Saturday, one of the leaders of the Philadelphia Church of Christ—Walter Elliot, who had given me "Revolution Through Restoration"—attended an Easter vigil service with me at St. Mary's Episcopal Church, Bainbridge Street. At several points in the service, Elliot seemed nervous, although he treated people at St. Mary's politely, even warmly.

The priest was a woman. The singing was rather restrained, and the sermon was short. Parts of the service were beautiful, and there was not much emphasis on winning souls. My girlfriend was also a member of St. Mary's. We were clearly planning to get together after the service; we might well have been planning to spend the night. The congregation, mostly black, greeted Elliot and me warmly. About 25 people were there, and I felt that St. Mary's, when viewed through Elliot's eyes, was a tiny and powerless institution.

The next morning (Easter Sunday), I went to the First Baptist Church of Philadelphia. Located in Rittenhouse Square, this church was one of the institutions from which the Philadelphia Church of Christ sometimes rented space in which to hold its meetings.

I found the service at First Baptist depressing. At several points, some people in the congregation said "amen" to something that had been sung or said. Those who did so were glared at—at least, so it seemed to me—by some others in the congregation, which was mostly white, fairly old, and quite prosperous. The pastor was a man, but the head of deacons was a woman. Some of the people were probably gay, for the church emphasized that gays were welcome.

The music—a lot of Handel, performed very professionally—was acceptable but not inspiring. The sermon, preached by a man with a doctorate, focused on the "message of Easter," which consisted, more or less entirely, of this: "People who don't want to be afraid don't have to be." The one or two jokes the preacher attempted fell flat. I remember thinking at the time that if this church is representative of mainstream Protestantism, one sees why Bible-carrying Christians do not have much respect for it.[14] The people at the First Baptist Church seemed enfeebled; the church itself seemed no more powerful than St. Mary's.

On the other hand, the services I attended at the Philadelphia Church of Christ made me feel that it was a power-filled institution. During the course of my fieldwork there, I found myself thinking a great deal about a claim that I had sometimes encountered in the scholarly literature on religious organizations: participation in religious organizations is empowering.[15]

Much of the power and authority created at the church was used to meet the institutional needs of the congregation itself and those of the movement of which it was a part. But some of the power created there flowed back to the members of the congregation. The Philadelphia Church of Christ did indeed give its members access to forms of power that they did not have access to the secular world. To the congregation, the "kingdom of God" was paired with and juxtaposed against "the world," which—among other things—posed a set of severe obstacles to those who wanted to follow God's will. Indeed, the people thought that the world was hostile to an individual who was really trying to follow Jesus.[16]

One of the sermons I heard suggested that when seen through the eyes of the world, a person who was really trying to follow Jesus might well appear to be a "Bible geek." Another sermon suggested that whenever a religious person mentioned the name of Jesus in a conversation that conformed to the rules of the world, the conversation was likely to come to a halt. A third talked about the ways in which the larger world "laughed at" and "ridiculed" Christians. A talk by one of the leaders of the movement asserted that the world is likely to view Christians who take Genesis more seriously than Darwin as "stupid," "ignorant," or even "insane." A woman in the congregation told me once—in the course of an informal conversation—that her experiences had taught her that disciples who didn't keep their religious views to themselves in a college classroom were likely to be told to stop wasting the class's time on God.[17]

But I do not mean to give the impression that the only reason the people at the Philadelphia Church of Christ viewed the world with suspicion was that it seemed to them to be hostile to those who were genuinely religious. That was not the case. When I was doing my fieldwork there, many members of the congregation were leading lives that would have been difficult *even if they did not have to face the peculiar challenges of living a Christian life in a world that was pictured as being quite thoroughly un-Christian.*

In the discourse of that church, the world was presented as a place where the members of the church were in danger of being oppressed. They lived the sorts of lives that could cause them to conclude, as a sermon preached by Walter Elliot put it, that it was their "lot in life" to be "kicked around and abused." Another sermon, preached by a man named Douglas Amherst, noted that it seemed natural to view the world as "oppressive"—that is, as a source of difficulties and stress. A third, preached by Kip McKean, noted that the world did not think that people like those who had come together (at a service sponsored by the church) to hear him speak were of any real importance. "The world tells us," he said, that "you are a nobody."

In the discourse of the Philadelphia Church of Christ, the move from powerlessness to power was presented as simple and direct. The people were told that "we don't have to be the losers we were in the world." All we had to do was to become a member of the church and to take the church's teachings about following Christ seriously. If we did that, God would take us from "a losing life to a winning life."

I cannot say definitely whether people in the congregation were really empowered. But I can say that the claim did have a good deal of plausibility, especially if what one means by "empowerment" is placing people in a situation that is likely to improve their self-esteem. The members of the Philadelphia Church of Christ were told that God wanted "great things" for them, that God had hand-picked a particular destiny for each one of them and that each of those destinies was a "grand" one.

The claim is especially plausible, too, if what one means by "empowerment" is feeling connected to a group made up of people who seem to be successful. The people I met at the church took great pride in knowing that men who were not at all effeminate—men like Cory Blackwell, a great athlete who had played in the National Basketball Association—were affiliated with their movement. They were proud, too, that beautiful women—women like Cory Blackwell's wife, who was reportedly paid $15,000 a day when she worked as a model—were members of the movement. And the people were also proud of the fact that a number of highly intelligent people—people with degrees from schools like Duke, Harvard, and the Massachusetts Institute of Technology—were a part of the movement with which they were connected. Sitting in a worship service at the Philadelphia Church of Christ, one could feel confident that Christians were not all stupid or ugly or dumb. One knew, as one of the leaders of the church told me in another context, that Christians were not simply "a bunch of losers."

So in some respects, my fieldwork at the church tended to confirm the claim that religious movements are empowering. But the fact that there is good reason to believe that participation in religious movements empowers people does not, of course, imply that religious movements usually foster power relations that are symmetrical. Consider, for instance, the band made up of the sons and daughters of people who had been oppressed slaves in Egypt. According to biblical accounts, the religion practiced by the Hebrews in Egypt was empowering. It helped them conspire together to escape Pharaoh's dominion. But from the position of the Canaanites, whom the band of Hebrews massacred, it is not at all clear that the religious practices of the Hebrews were empowering. Empowering to whom? From the perspective of the Canaanites, the Exodus story reads like the prelude to a saga that celebrates bloody conquest.[18]

A similar argument could, of course, be made about the religious movement associated with Jesus. The Christian Scriptures make it clear that the movement founded by the followers of Jesus was empowering. It convinced them and then helped them demonstrate that the Pontius Pilates of this world do not always win. But from the perspective of the "stubborn" and "blind" Jews we hear so much about in Christian Scriptures—and from that of their descendants—it is not at all clear that the religious practices of the followers of Jesus were empowering. Empowering to whom? From such perspectives, the stories that are told about Jesus' first followers might sound like the first section of a long narrative that ends in bloody conquest. It is not all that far from "the Great Commission," which is recorded in the last chapter of the Gospel of Matthew, to the vision ("by this sign conquer") that gave Constantine's armies a Christian emblem under which to march.[19]

We cannot, then, assume that religious movements that empower people eschew all asymmetric power relations. In fact, it is not impossible to conceive of a situation in which a religious movement that empowered people could be at the same time a movement that was determined to conquer and subdue the rest of the world. Indeed, the movement with which the Philadelphia Church of Christ was associated was, I believe, just such a movement. By the time I had completed my fieldwork there, I realized that the movement was something akin to a military organization devoted to foreign conquest.

This view was largely the result of things I had seen and heard during my fieldwork. I was invited on an expedition to the Pocono Mountains with a group of men from the congregation to participate in war games (the guns shot paint bombs, not real bullets). I participated in services that concluded with hundreds of voices singing with great vigor and considerable skill a song that celebrated the fact that God's terrible swift sword had been unleashed. I heard reports on conferences where the leaders of the movement had met to talk about "world conquest." I heard a man who spent a lot of time in prayer praised as a great "prayer warrior." I heard a Bible compared, in a way I found a little terrifying, to a "pocketknife."

My view of the Philadelphia Church of Christ as one unit of an army that was devoted to establishing a worldwide empire was also the result of reading a piece of literature—a book called *Bent on Conquest*—that people from the church sold me and encouraged me to read. At many of the meetings, there was a literature table manned by several members of the congregation. The literature wasn't free, but it wasn't terribly expensive either. Three dollars was all it took to purchase *Bent on Conquest*. Written by Andrew Giambarba and published in 1988, it described and analyzed an attempt by the International Churches of Christ (Boston Movement) to evangelize Mexico City. One of the starting points was Giambarba's realization that "the battleground of history is littered with the corpses of failed movements." Another was his declaration that the movement of which he was a part was determined not to become another corpse.[20]

That fate could be avoided, he argued, if the movement courageously lived out the Great Commission. Giambara said that the Great Commission should be read as a Christian "disciple's marching orders." Readers were told that they should think of the Great Commission as "a command" given to the "troops" by the "general" himself. "These orders," Giambara emphasized, "are not open to debate" (p. 7). Following them faithfully would produce great results: "As we obey His [the Almighty's] call and make disciples of all nations in this generation, we need not fear anything. Our Lord is leading and we will go forth as conquerors" (p. 98).

Giambarba presented the effort to make converts in Mexico City as a campaign undertaken by a small but dedicated band of disciples "to conquer a foreign city" (p. 44). That band of disciples—made up, as Giambarba noted in passing, of "thirteen non-Mexicans"—did not want to do any "meddling in international politics" and certainly did not desire "worldly . . . power." Nevertheless, the disciples had firmly determined that they would be "world leaders"; they would lead the world in a way that was different from, but analogous to, the way in which men like Mahatma Gandhi and John F. Kennedy led the world. The band of disciples was determined to "make history" (p. 48).

According to Giambarba, there was no real doubt in their minds that they would do so, for they knew that God had "given" Mexico City to them as the Lord had "given" Jericho to the Israelite troops whom Joshua commanded (p. 44). I found this passage of Giambarba's pamphlet particularly disturbing. I recalled that after the Israelites "took" the city that God had "given" them, nearly everything in it was consumed by fire. All but a handful of the residents were put to death.[21]

OBEDIENT DISCIPLES

In April 1992, I took two of the ministers of the Church of Christ to the first game of the Philadelphia Phillies' 1992 season. When we got to the ballpark, it became clear that there had been a minor mixup with our tickets. It looked as though we were going to spend a lot of time in a slow-moving line before we could get the tickets we had ordered. It seemed as if we would miss the first inning, and all three of us were annoyed. One of the ministers made a joke of the situation, saying something like this: "Well, I am sure that they will let us cut in line if we tell them that we are ministers of the gospel."

We didn't, of course, do that, and I wonder what would have happened if we had tried. Jeers? (Philadelphia fans did, in fact, boo Santa Claus on one occasion.) Shoving? Puzzlement? In many circumstances, this claim would simply seem too bizarre to comprehend. In the public meetings of the Philadelphia Church of Christ, however, such claims were not at all strange. I was struck by how much authority the leaders of the church exercised over the rest of the membership, as was Bruce Comens, although the way in which authority was exercised at the first meeting that I attended and at the two that Bruce Comens attended was by no means the same.

Moreover, at another meeting, I wrote the following: "It would be hard to imagine a less democratic presentation. What mattered? The Bible. Which verses? The verses to which [the minister who was teaching us how to win converts] directed our attention. What did those verses mean? What he said they meant." My fieldnotes contain a good many entries like this, but I won't reproduce any more of them here. The basic point is a simple one: the public rituals at the Philadelphia Church of Christ were based on the assumption that it was natural for laypeople to defer to ministers. The naturalization of that sort of deference was at the heart of those meetings.[22]

The Church of Christ's emphasis on authority was not by any means limited to public meetings. It was, rather, a defining characteric of the congregation's day-to-day existence. In the course of my fieldwork, I came to realize that each member of the church was being "discipled" by someone else. The chain of discipling partnerships linked each member directly to the ministers of the church. Since I never became a link in that chain, I don't really have any direct knowledge of how the process worked. I did, however, learn a little about it from people who were personally involved.

The relationship between discipling partners was explicitly hierarchical. People who were being discipled had *no* authority over the people who were discipling them. People who were discipling others had a *huge* amount of authority over people whom they were discipling. In the past, I was told, the movement had come close to saying that one had to do whatever one's discipler said. One of the leaders of the movement is reported to have said that when his discipler told him, "Brother, you do this," he never allowed himself to "argue" against the direction or even to "question" it. Instead he always responded with a simple, clear word: "Okay." It was crucial, he asserted, for all Christians who want to be "effective for God" to live lives that are characterized by that sort of instantaneous obedience to the directions they received from their discipler.[23]

By the time of my fieldwork, the movement had retreated, in part at least, from that position. But it still expected a great deal of deference from the junior discipleship partner. And the movement still believed that it was illegitimate for a member to shield any aspect of his or her life from the surveillance of his or her discipler. One of the sermons I heard included a passage in which an imaginary member of the congregation was portrayed as asking: "Isn't anything private?" The answer was clear: "No."

Most of the members—perhaps *all* of the members—of the Philadelphia Church of Christ were aware that nonmembers were likely to find submission to the authority of disciplers odd or dangerous. In fact, this aspect of the church was often a focus in press reports that pictured the movement as "a dangerous religious cult."

So the people at the Church of Christ were not surprised when I asked them why their movement clung to a set of practices that had received so much criticism from outsiders. Although I never got a full answer to that question, on a number of occasions I was given an adumbration of it. The answer seemed to depend on two separate assertions. First, the movement's emphasis on discipling partnerships was one of the keys to its being able to "do things." Churches that are run by "big bureaucracies" and churches that are run by people who deeply believe in the importance of adhering to democratic principles often find it hard to "do anything." If the movement was going to accomplish its ultimate goals, it had to be sure to avoid such pitfalls. That assertion struck me as plausible.

The second assertion was that discipling partnerships were in keeping with biblical principles. To a much greater degree than most Americans realize, I was told, the practices of the Philadelphia Church of Christ were analogous to those in the Scriptures. Although I do not have much expertise in biblical studies, that assertion also seems plausible.[24]

LISTENING TO THE Bible study talks and reading literature distributed by the Philadelphia Church of Christ, I learned a good deal about how the members were taught to make converts. They were to treat potential converts in ways that closely paralleled how they treated me. That is, they were to invite potential converts to attend church with them, to play basketball with them, and to read the Bible with them under carefully controlled circumstances.

My suspicion is that nearly all the people who became members of the church knew a lot about Christianity before coming into contact with the group. From some perspectives, nearly all of them would have been described as at least nominally Christian before their "conversions." It was not entirely clear, therefore, how to interpret what occurred when someone underwent a conversion in the Church of Christ,[25] where there was a conversion only when the person agreed to become a link in the chain that was forged through discipling partnerships.

On a few occasions, people treated me as though I had become such a link. One of the leaders of the congregation actually introduced me to a visitor from a sister church as "a great basketball player and a mighty man of God." But, of course, I never really became one of the links in the chain, nor did I ever pretend to have done so. The repeated efforts made by the members to get me to submit to the discipling process failed.

I am now going to describe one of the attempts made by the church members to turn me into one of them. Doing so will shed some light on what it means to become a discipleship partner. The attempt was made by a man named Terry Calvert, who had been raised a Baptist. When I first met him he was probably in his early 30s. He was one of the leaders of the church, though not a particularly prominent one.

Calvert came from a relatively poor family. When he was a child, his mother had two jobs, one of which was cleaning a set of offices. She put Calvert and his siblings on her payroll, and Calvert was working as an office cleaner by the time he was 9. With financial help from his mother, Calvert attended college. After graduation, he worked for a bank in Cincinnati. Eventually, he was making $50,000 a year, but he left that job and became a missionary to India. His first year there his salary was $8,000. While he was in India, a person whom Calvert described as "a notorious fixer-upper" introduced him to a woman named Christine Singh. The two of them were soon wed and then moved to the United States. When I met Calvert, he and his wife were devoting a good deal of their attention to strengthening their marriage and to raising their young son.

Early in 1992, Calvert gave a brief talk at a worship service that I attended. I liked the talk and told him so after the service. Not long after that, on February 16, Calvert asked if I would like to get together to talk and to study the Bible. I said yes, and we arranged to meet four days later at my apartment. We talked perhaps for two hours.

Calvert did not waste a lot of time on small talk. He quickly steered the conversation to my spiritual condition and what the Bible could tell me about it. He asked me about the sort of work that I did and about the religious communities of which I was a part. He told me, without much prodding, that it did not seem to him as if I was living a worthwhile life: I was not really touching people or making disciples.

Calvert told me frankly that he had no good reason to suppose that I was really a Christian. I was an Episcopalian, and the Episcopal Church adhered to doctrines that were unscriptural. Moreover, by my own admission, I had not led anyone to Christ, which was probably a sign that I did not really believe what I said I believed. In this respect, he said, Protestants like me compared unfavorably with "fundamentalist Muslims." To him, the matter was pretty straightforward: if I really believed what I said I believed, I would try—"aggressively"—to get others to see the world as I did.

The more we talked, the more I suspected that Calvert thought nothing was as important for a Christian as "making disciples." Certainly working against nuclear war or for social justice was not nearly so important, nor were private prayer and corporate worship. Calvert believed that it was especially important for a Christian to try to convert famous people—athletes, movie stars, models—to the faith. I let Calvert know, not very politely, that I disagreed with him on this matter. I told him that focusing on the famous rather than the humble struck me as more "worldly" than "Christian."[26]

Calvert did not try to convince me that I was wrong. He did say, however, that from its earliest days the Christian church has especially rejoiced in winning successful people. Paul was "successful," as was the Ethiopian eunuch. He also said that it did not make much sense to take special delight in converting poor people: "It is easy to convert poor people. They are so needy." That comment, made in a contemptuous tone, suggested that bringing poor people to Christ was too easy to be interesting.

Calvert believed that the Bible has to be read as a simple book, one that contains practical answers to our problems. He thought that my readings of Scripture were "too academic" and "not practical enough." This theme came up perhaps a dozen times in the course of our conversation. He wanted me to see that the Bible is not nearly so hard a book to understand correctly as I thought it was. For instance, "repentance" is an easy word to understand, and if it weren't Christians would need to find a simple way of understanding it. Calvert's experience in India had taught him that you cannot preach an overly complex gospel if you want to convert people to Christianity.

Complications connected with understanding words or passages or books in the Scriptures were brushed aside or ignored. For example, as we talked about the relationship between "success" and Christianity, I mentioned that the oldest manuscripts of the Gospel of Mark didn't include the final verses of the last chapter (which means, among other things, that they don't include any straightforward accounts of resurrection appearances). Calvert did not express any direct disagreement with that point. Rather, he began to ask a series of pointed questions to be sure I believed that the Bible was inspired. He even asked me if the English translations were inspired. (I believe that the answer he wanted to hear was yes.) At that point, I became impatient. "Come on," I said. "Are you asking me if the committee that translated the NIV[27] was inspired by God in some supernatural way? That seems silly. Of course I do not believe that."

So, as you can see, Calvert and I quarreled a good deal, often because of our differing understanding of authority. From my point of view, Calvert was continually using a set of techniques designed to get me to submit to his authority. He wanted me to realize that it was natural for him to be the "authoritative teacher" and for me to be the "humble student." It wasn't clear to me what the warrant for that belief was, although it seemed to have something to do with having been ordained a minister of the gospel and with knowing more about the Bible than I did.[28]

Throughout our conversations, Calvert would ask me "simple questions" or perhaps "rhetorical questions" about the Christian faith in general and the Bible in particular. I tried to provide the best answers I could, which were almost always judged to be wrong. Wrong answers seemed to exasperate Calvert.

At some point in the session, I let Calvert know, quite directly, that I suspected that the people in his church made a determined effort to use the Scriptures to buttress their own authority. I suspected, I said, that they plotted to get whomever they were talking to to agree to "what the Scriptures say about themselves" (this phrase, one that Calvert had used with me, concerned the authority possessed by the Scriptures). Then they tried get the person to whom they were talking to think that the Scriptures have to be read the way in which they were read at the Philadelphia Church of Christ. Finally, they told the person that anytime he or she disagreed with them about anything, he or she was going against the will of God.

Calvert responded by saying that my analysis was just wrong, and he used what had occurred during our session to make the point. I had been picking and choosing Scriptures. I had been interpreting them. He had not been doing that. He was just trying to teach me what the Scriptures said for themselves.[29]

Near the end of the session, Calvert made the ground rules he thought we were playing by quite explicit. If we were going to continue to talk to each other about the Bible, we had to agree on two points. First, we had to accept the fact that he was the teacher and I was the student. He was not there to learn from me; I was there to learn from him. Second, we were going to have to agree that I was not a Christian. Unless these facts were recognized, he said, we were unlikely to make much progress.

Calvert and I never again tried to read the Bible together. When we saw each other at a worship service we tried to be nice, but we never succeeded in having another serious conversation. We were polite to each other but not much more.

LAW-ABIDING CONSUMERS

The Philadelphia Church of Christ did not ask its members to forgo the pleasures offered by consumer goods. A number of the people enjoyed a way of life that depended on an almost embarrassingly high rate of consumption. But the church did not formally embrace the school of theology—prosperity theology—that emphasizes the economic rewards of embracing Christianity. And on at least one occasion, I heard what sounded to me like a straightforward criticism of this school. McKean asserted, the one time I heard him preach, that the "radio and TV preachers" who said that "accepting Jesus will make you rich" were mistaken. That way of looking at the world was, McKean claimed, unbiblical. The Bible did not assure us that people who followed Jesus would necessarily achieve success in a society as thoroughly commercial as the contemporary United States.

The Church of Christ taught its members that the consumer goods that commercial success makes available are not, in any case, *finally* satisfying. One talk I heard asserted, for example: "We Americans are surrounded by things that will not last. The things that we have worked for fade away." Americans devoted a large proportion of their lives to acquiring things—such as a car, a house, and "a comfortable lifestyle"— that could not possibly bring them ultimate satisfaction. Another talk emphasized that Americans often amassed enough wealth to live as if wearing Rolexes was natural, whereas their lives were characterized by a "terrible emptiness." Economic success was not seen at the Church of Christ as necessarily fulfilling.

This somewhat skeptical appraisal of the rewards of economic success was accompanied by a tendency (a tendency evident in many different aspects of the life of the movement of which the church was a part) to encourage people to act in ways that were—when judged strictly from the standpoint of commerce—somewhat "irrational."[30] I heard stories about people in the wider movement who had given up good jobs to move to other cities, cities where the movement needed them and where they would be paid poorly. I heard other stories about people who had given up good jobs because the jobs prevented them from attending meetings sponsored by the movement as often as they would like.

These sorts of financial sacrifices were relatively rare, but it was quite common for people to devote a great deal of their time—perhaps twenty hours a week—to such economically "irrational" activities as prayer, Bible reading, and public worship services sponsored by the church. It also was quite common for people to give a lot of their money—perhaps 15 to 25 percent of their annual income—to the church.[31]

Much of this money funded ministries that were especially directed at the poor. Nearly every worship service I attended at the Philadelphia Church of Christ included a collection for such ministries. These collections were often accompanied by talks that asserted, in quite strong terms, that God expected those who were relatively rich to devote a good deal of their wealth to meeting the material needs of the poor.

However, although the people were quite willing to support ministries aimed at the poor, they also had concluded that there is a real sense in which it is "up to the poor to help themselves."[32] They sometimes evinced impatience with people who refused to take advantage of the opportunities offered to them by living in a free market society. Moreover, they often talked about evangelization as though they thought it would be a mistake for the church to devote its energy to converting the poor. The souls of people who were not poor were not *really* seen as more valuable than the souls of people who were. But converting poor people—or at least too many poor people—could easily distract the movement from its goal of world conquest. A focus on "poor people" was a "temptation" that had to be avoided.[33]

The products created by Hollywood movies, professional sports, television, radio, and popular music were not seen as a "temptation" at the Philadelphia Church of Christ. The people did not make a particular effort to prevent such products from influencing the way in which they viewed the world or ran their worship services. It was understood that everyone knew a great deal about such products, and someone who did not would have found much of what was done and said at the church mystifying. To understand the worship services, one had to know about the videos shown on MTV; the articles in *Sports Illustrated*; the movies about Indiana Jones and Rocky Balboa; the songs sung by Stevie Wonder, Simon and Garfunkel, Garth Brooks, and Lou Reed; the sorts of jokes told by comedians like David Letterman; and the commercials shown on television.

Nearly all the people at the church did know a great deal about the world of commercial entertainment. When one of the leaders analyzed the spiritual journey of a disciple according to the categories in the lyrics of rock-and-roll and country songs, his audience seemed to know exactly what he meant. When another leader exhorted his listeners to be followers of Christ in language drawn from commercials that hawked the American Express Gold Card, nobody in the room looked puzzled or confused. So the fact that the language used at the church was drawn very largely from the entertainment industry did not seem to limit the capacity of its leaders to communicate their ideas clearly to the members. But it did seem to limit the leaders' capacity to address certain issues and to make certain points. To a remarkable degree, the products manufactured by the culture industries controlled what was sayable at the church.[34]

The people at the Church of Christ believed that Christians should strive to avoid needless confrontations with the state. Although the church did not have a consensus on what was "needless" and what was "unavoidable," "needless" was generally defined quite broadly. In practice it included, for example, nearly all the kinds of confrontations that Mennonites in the United States have run into. One of the women Dwyer-McNulty interviewed—Emma Roberts—told her, for instance, that it was just plain "ridiculous" for Christians to refuse to pay some or all of their taxes. Roberts also told Dwyer-McNulty that Christians should teach their children "that there are times when it's necessary to fight for your country."[35] Terry Calvert told me that the Bible teaches Christians to disobey government authorities only when those authorities explicitly prohibit the free exercise of religion. He thought that people who believe that Christians have a duty to oppose tyrants like Hitler had misunderstood the Scriptures.[36] Walter Elliot understood "needless confrontations" more narrowly. He told me that he could imagine the Bible leading a Christian toward becoming a conscientious objector to military service. But he also could easily imagine a Christian deciding instead that it was perfectly appropriate to make a living in the armed forces.

As far as I know, I never met a person who was a conscientious objector while I was doing my fieldwork at the Philadelphia Church of Christ, nor did I meet a war-tax resister. The people at the church had no *particular* commitment to resisting the war-making power of modern nation-states. It just wasn't a matter to which they devoted a great deal of attention.

The church did, of course, pay a great deal of attention to making converts, and its proselytizing sometimes led to trouble with government officials. A zoning board in one of the suburbs of Philadelphia, for example, briefly considered prohibiting two of the church leaders who lived there from holding Bible studies in their home. The board was concerned that the house might be used to convert innocent women and men into a cult. Also, some administrators at Temple University—Philadelphia's largest state-related university—tried to minimize contacts between the church and the student body. The administrators didn't want Temple students to be duped into joining the church, and they wanted to make sure that Temple's regulations for student organizations and activities prevented that from happening.[37]

Although I did not learn all I wanted to about how the people at the Church of Christ responded to such tensions between themselves and the representatives of the state, I believe that they never suspected that the tensions were produced by their own wrongdoing. They were more likely to see the problem as the result of an anti-Christian bias on the part of the state. They were certain, moreover, that religious liberty, properly understood, included "aggressive" evangelism; no government agency had the right to obstruct it.

Clinging to such beliefs gave the people some leverage against the tendency of nation-states to naturalize their own authority, and their consistent refusal to conflate the United States with the kingdom of God probably gave them more. The members of the church drew a very clear line between the kingdom of God and the United States in the literature they distributed, the songs they sang, and the sermons they preached. Their rituals during services almost never sacralized the state, although

American flags were occasionally present in the rooms where they worshiped. But flags were never objects of devotion; in fact they were almost always simply ignored. The American flag did not matter a great deal while a person was worshiping God.

The church taught its members that the nation-state was not likely to solve the problems that confronted them and people like them. People with problems, the church taught, should fix their eyes on the kingdom of God. Looking to the state for help was, in a fundamental sense, simply a waste of time.

The Philadelphia Church of Christ taught that in the final analysis all social ills are spiritual ills and that it therefore makes no sense to try to solve spiritual problems through state action.[38] Thus Christians ought not to become entangled in the state. They should pay their taxes and vote for the candidate of their choice, but that was about all. Certainly the church did not believe that Christians should pour much of their energy into political activity. Politics was not what the gospel was primarily about. The church encouraged its members to believe that politics was, as Mather said, "kind of hopeless."[39] So the members of the congregation did not try to get the state to improve the services it provides to poor people or to people who are ill. Indeed they almost went out of their way to avoid getting caught up in that sort of distracting political activity.

PASSIONATE COUNTERFEMINISTS

The church people also did not join in political activities aimed at making the U.S. populace conform more closely to their standards of sexual morality. The members of the Philadelphia Church of Christ believed that fornication, adultery, sodomy, and abortion were appalling sins, but they did not see any point in trying to use legislation to improve the nation's moral climate. They certainly did not devote much of their energy toward lobbying for laws to prohibit "unbiblical sex."[40]

Heterosexual norms were not enforced as passionately at the Philadelphia Church of Christ as they were at some other churches in the United States in the 1990s. I heard only a few remarks from the leaders of the Philadelphia Church of Christ concerning the evils of homosexuality. *None* explicitly recommended that Christians try hard to have the state uphold "traditional family values." The church was not going to serve as a base from which political campaigns aimed at using the state to discriminate against lesbians and gay men were going to be launched.

Nevertheless, the church enforced heterosexual norms quite strictly, and its members were absolutely sure that God disapproved of homosexuality. Emma Roberts, for instance, expressed considerable disgust with a story she had read in the *Inquirer* about a congregation of gay Christians. She said that although God loves such people, they have to realize that "God definitely wants [them] to recognize that homosexuality is wrong." There was no place in the church for unrepentant homosexuals.

In fact, all the members of the church were sure that God disapproved of *all* sexual relations that did not take place in the context of a heterosexual marriage. Both Emma Roberts and Sarah Mather talked to Dwyer-McNulty at some length, for example, about the church's emphasis on "keeping 'pure'" before marriage. Both told her that the movement of which the church was a part had strict rules to keep its members from putting themselves into situations that might lead to sexual immorality. Again and again I heard people emphasize the divergence between the sexual promiscuity in "the world" and the sexual "purity" that was fostered and protected by the church and the movement.

The Philadelphia Church of Christ, however, was not afraid of or hostile to sexual desire per se. Indeed, it supported courtship rituals that would produce lifelong heterosexual unions in which sexual desire could be properly, and passionately, expressed. Sometimes the courtship rituals at the church were so intense that they led to something like a "dating frenzy."[41] All the women in the church who were not *actual* wives were sometimes seen as *potential* wives. Sometimes, too, all the men were seen as either actual or potential husbands. The point of the dating frenzy was to see that such potential did not go to waste.

The Church of Christ also made great efforts to maintain the heterosexual unions that were produced by the dating frenzies it fostered. Time and again I ran into people whose marriages the leaders of the church were trying to preserve, strengthen, and improve. Couples who were living in cities that seemed to put strains on their marriage were encouraged to move elsewhere. Couples whose difficulties were thought to stem from a failure to understand and follow the biblical principles that governed Christian marriages were given intensive counseling. The people believed that these efforts worked remarkably well. As already mentioned, one of the men actually claimed that "we have *never* had a divorce with couples who have remained faithful to God and his church."[42]

I am not sure that Emma Roberts would have been willing to make such a sweeping claim. But she, too, emphasized what a wonderful job the church did in fostering strong marriages. When she was asked, for example: "Do you think that your church has something to offer women they can't get elsewhere?" her reply centered on how "wonderful and affectionate" her marriage was and how well she and her husband communicated. She believed that in the outside world such marriages—and such husbands—were quite rare.[43]

The members of the Church of Christ believed that the roles of husbands and wives in particular and men and women in general should be distinct. Blurred roles were a violation of God's laws: "God created very specific roles for men and women"; a follower of Jesus had a duty to learn just what those roles were and then be sure to fit into them.[44] For example, throughout the movement women were taught that it was "very important" for them to stay "at home for the children." Women had also been taught that it was important to defer to the authority of their husbands: "It says in the Bible that women must submit to and respect their husbands" and that women submitting to their husbands' authority made marriage "easier." Marriages were strengthened, they thought, by their knowing that the husband was "the boss."[45]

"Boss" is perhaps a slightly misleading word in this context. At the Philadelphia Church of Christ, husbands were expected to love their wives (bosses don't have to love their workers). But it would be difficult to exaggerate how central a role the headship of the husband played in the domestic ideology of the church. It would also be difficult to overstate how central a role the husband-as-boss idea played in the marriage counseling that the church sponsored. On some occasions, at least, the leaders of the church implied that getting wives to recognize their husbands' authority was fully one-half of what marital counseling was all about. All a Christian counselor had to do, it was sometimes claimed, was to tell husbands to love their wives and tell wives to obey their husbands. Giving that sort of advice—and making sure that it was followed—always solved whatever problems couples might be experiencing.

As you would expect, the directions the women received were not limited to matters of obedience. Rather, they covered a wide range of topics, including, for example, physical appearance. Sarah Mather's conversation with Dwyer-McNulty made it clear that women in the movement were given a great deal of "encouragement to be as beautiful" as they possibly could, to "make the most of what [they] had." In addition, the women were supposed to be thin. Mather said that during her early involvement in the church she had gotten the impression that if a woman were not a size 8 or 9 or if she were 5 pounds overweight, the members of the church would consider her to be a "bad" woman. Mather herself had felt "condemned" on occasions when she had eaten in the presence of another member of the church, one who had very particular standards about what Christian women should look like.[46]

I want to be clear here. My argument is simply that in the Philadelphia Church of Christ, patriarchal norms were enforced. It is *not* that all the effects of this enforcement were, from all possible perspectives, pernicious. In reality, my fieldnotes contain material that could be used to construct an argument that the church enforced a set of patriarchal norms in ways that empowered its members.[47] Children in the congregation were given a lot of material and emotional support. Fathers devoted a good deal of their time to their daughters and sons.

Moreover, many of the marriages I encountered at the church seemed quite loving, and some of the couples I met took understandable pride in being able to establish stable relationships in the midst of quite brutal economic circumstances.[48] One cannot argue that because the church strictly enforced patriarchal norms, its members were stripped of all the tactics that give people agency, but the range of tactics that could be employed was quite constricted. It is this constriction that I want to emphasize.

I also want to emphasize—as will become clear shortly—the degree to which the church limited the roles women could play within the congregation. However, I also want to note that women were given a lot of responsibility. At the Church of Christ, women were given positions as "counselors" whose spiritual authority was somewhat analogous to that of male ministers. These counselors were paid salaries by the church so they would not have to work in a secular job; the church did not want a secular job to distract the counselors from the ministry that God had assigned them.

Some of the counselors had a lot of power. Indeed, during my field-work, the person at the church who had played the most important role in shaping the development of the movement with which it was associated was not a male minister but a woman counselor—Pat Guthrie.[49] Guthrie and the other counselors gave formal talks before large groups of other women who had gathered to study the Bible. They also created networks of "discipling partnerships" and Bible-study groups, which were made up entirely of women and which were free, to some degree, at least, from direct male supervision.[50]

Belonging to such networks gave the women a lot of personal power and protection. Roberts and Mather both talked about their lives in ways that emphasized that fact, as did other women associated with the church. I was told, for example, that if a woman who belonged to one of these networks was being abused in any way by her husband, she could tell her sisters and receive counseling and help. Her sisters would make sure that the abuse stopped.

But the female networks of discipling partnerships and Bible-study groups were not places in which the patriarchal elements of the Christian tradition could be criticized. The tendency of Christians to think of God as masculine was not questioned, nor was the possibility that the women might want to learn more about feminist or womanist theologies, which weren't on the map at the Philadelphia Church of Christ. And though the women counselors were—from some points of view—quite powerful, they did not have much autonomy from the men who ran the church or the movement. At one time in the history of the movement, the only way a woman could become a counselor was to marry a minister. The women knew, as Mather told Dwyer-McNulty, that "if you got one [that is, if you were able to convince a minister to marry you], then as his wife you could have an important role in the church as a women's counselor." At that time, a woman in the movement who failed to make such a match had to be content with other, more mundane forms of service.

Later on in the history of the International Churches of Christ (Boston Movement), some women who were not married to ministers were allowed to become counselors. But the basic pattern of a counselor's authority, depending in large part on the power and prestige of her husband, was never completely destroyed. Even during my fieldwork, some of the counselors were serving as simple auxiliaries to their husbands' ministry. I sometimes thought that they devoted much of their lives to making sure that the women under their supervision acted as their husbands thought they should.

Throughout its history, the movement has taught its members that the practice of making women into "ministers" of the gospel rather than into "counselors" was something that no church with a proper understanding of the Bible would ever consider doing. Neither Dwyer-McNulty nor I ever encountered any women at the church who thought otherwise. In reality, the impermissibility of ordaining women as ministers was one of the topics about which women spoke most passionately and most emphatically.[51] They were absolutely sure, they said, that "women ministers aren't in God's plan."[52]

At the Philadelphia Church of Christ, God's plan seemed to prohibit women from performing a wide range of ecclesiastical duties. They could not preside at communion. They could not distribute consecrated bread or wine to the members of the congregation. They could not even serve as ushers. And, in general, the church did not allow women to speak during public worship services that were attended by both women and men. Women were never permitted to preach, to deliver informal talks, or to read the Scriptures aloud during such services. In fact, I can remember only one occasion in the course of my fieldwork in which a woman spoke in a meeting. After hearing a talk about how Christians should think about the theory of evolution, a young woman raised her hand and asked the speaker a short question. His reply consisted largely of condescending jokes.

SEVEN

CONCLUSION

MY FIELDWORK CHANGED the way in which I thought about Bible-carrying Christians and myself. Like many other academics, I am most comfortable when I can emphasize the distance that separates me from them. I feel most comfortable when I can draw a sharp line between what they do and what I do. But by the time I had concluded my fieldwork, I was less struck by what separated us than by what we had in common. How they lived their lives and how I lived mine had both been decisively shaped by the traditions of Protestant Christianity in the United States. We had far more in common with each other than either they or I had in common with people who had been decisively shaped by the traditions of neopaganism or rabbinic Judaism. Whatever tendencies I might have had to see Bible-carrying Christians as "the other" had been worn down by the time the project came to a close.

At the same time, my fieldwork also made it hard for me to produce analyses of Bible-carrying Christians that deemphasized the links between their churches and asymmetric power relations, which I emphasize here more than in another book I wrote on this general topic: *A Transforming Faith*. That is in part because my first book was based on reading texts rather than on fieldwork. It is one thing to read a diatribe against homosexuals and another to hear it; similarly, reading about a Bible-based crusade to conquer the world for Christ is very different from being subjected to one. In any case, by the time I had finished my fieldwork for this book I had come to believe that the links between Bible-carrying Christian churches and certain forms of asymmetric power relations are stronger and more resilient than I had previously suspected.

I met many Bible-carrying Christians who consistently deferred to the wishes and opinions of their pastors—with great regularity at the Philadelphia Church of Christ and with some frequency at Oak Grove.

At both of those churches, respect for ministers of the gospel seemed to be more important than respect for the ideals of modern democracy.

At all three churches, people rarely stepped outside the confines of patriarchal norms. Even at the Philadelphia Mennonite Fellowship, people believed that in a fundamental sense it is natural for the feminine to defer to the masculine. And this belief was not simply the result of unthinking prejudice. It rested on a way of understanding and describing the nature of the universe that had been drawn from the Bible. The Bible, as it was read in all three of these congregations, made it clear that it is unnatural to think of the redeemer of the world as a woman. It made it clear, too, that the reality that created and sustains the universe must be thought of as God and not as Goddess; as King, not Queen.

The ways in which the Bible was read at all three congregations emphasized that practices that do not lie within heterosexual norms are essentially ungodly. Homosexuals were sometimes regarded primarily as sinners who ought to be treated with compassionate tolerance. At other times they were seen as laughable failures or as abhorrent deviants. Marginalization did not rest on simple prejudice. It rested rather on an carefully worked-out set of axioms and arguments in which "God" provided the warrants for discriminating against those who do not conform to heterosexual norms. Indeed, in the Bible-carrying Christian churches I studied, that was one of the most important things that "God" did.

In two of the churches, a deep commitment to God's laws was sometimes accompanied by a willingness—an eagerness, even—to acquiesce to the claims of corporations and of the state. Oak Grove, for example, was full of people who were determined to protect the interests of "the free enterprise system" and of the United States of America. At the Philadelphia Church of Christ, the authority of business corporations was seldom criticized and was often taken for granted. Indeed, in some respects the practices and attitudes in that congregation seemed even more consistently commercial than those at Oak Grove. And the importance of deferring, except in the most extreme situations, to the authority of the state was emphasized repeatedly.

But at the Church of Christ, the tendency of the U.S. government to make its authority seem natural and unquestionable was sometimes resisted. The people drew a sharp line between the kingdom of God and the state, and their ultimate allegiance was to God's kingdom rather than to any civil government. Even at Oak Grove, a congregation where the links between Bible-carrying Christianity and asymmetrical power relations were often particularly obvious, I sometimes encountered assumptions and beliefs that were quite different from those that infuse for-profit corporations and the state.

At the Philadelphia Mennonite Fellowship, the power of the state and for-profit corporations was often resisted. The Mennonites' resistance was evident in the way they raised money, ran their business meetings, treated eaach other, and conducted their worship services. The people employed a remarkably wide range of tactics to keep themselves from simply assuming that the practices and worldviews that are congruent with states and corporations are "natural" and those that are not are bizarre. These tactics certainly did not work perfectly, but they were, as often as not, startlingly effective. For that reason, I sometimes envied the Mennonites. More than once I suspected that the congregation did a better job of resisting the authority of modern nation-states and for-profit corporations than did *any* of the educational institutions, museums, unions, political parties, publishing enterprises, scholarly organizations, and religious groups with which I was associated.

I did not think that Bible-carrying Christian churches were able to resist the claims of states and corporations *despite* their attachment to the Bible. It would be more accurate to say that the congregations' attachment to Bible-carrying Christianity was a large part of what made them question such claims.

The texts that were brought together to form the Bible were produced in social settings that were astoundingly different from those that prevail in contemporary North America. The gap between those social settings and ours creates the possibility of seeing the latter as less than natural. So when people join Bible-carrying Christian communities, they are joining organizations in which it is sometimes possible to use the leverage provided by the Christian Scriptures to denaturalize the authority of corporations and states. Such delegitimations are not natural or inevitable, but neither are they terribly difficult to achieve. It is not hard to read the Bible in ways that destabilize the authority of corporations, and states. For that reason, Bible-carrying Christians are sometimes able to envision a reality that is not circumscribed by the dictates of corporations or states.

That this can occur is a large part of what makes these congregations interesting politically. There are relatively few places in contemporary America where the claims of corporations and the state are interrogated thoughtfully and radically, but it does sometimes occur in Bible-carrying Christian churches. Although this means that some of these congregations are queer, peculiar, and outlandish, it also means that they are, in spite of everything, important and valuable.

This brings to mind an episode in a novella that is largely concerned with Bible-carrying Christians in the American South: Flannery O'Connor's *Wise Blood*. The protagonist—a man named Hazel Motes—engages in devotional practices that his landlady finds terribly excessive. They really are, by nearly all standards of judgment, quite horrifying. His landlady tells him that what he is doing is "not normal." "It's like one of them gory stories, it's something that people have quit doing—like boiling in oil or being a saint or walling up cats," she said. "There's no reason for it. People have quit doing it." He replies: "They ain't quit doing it, as long as I'm doing it."

Motes's argument is hard to refute. A similar one could be made by some Bible-carrying Christians. It is, someone might say, impossible to resist the authority of modern nation-states and for-profit corporations. "They" have won; "we" have lost. This is the sort of argument that the heads of some religious, educational, and artistic organizations in the contemporary United States would make. "We are living," they might say, "in a world that is largely defined by states and markets. Those of us who are concerned with practical matters have all had to quit acting as though that weren't so."

"We haven't all decided to quit," some Bible-carrying Christians could say, "as long as we're still doing it." Such Christians don't have any guarantees that they will win. It would, in fact, be easy to exaggerate the degree to which they have agency of any sort. Still: "We haven't all decided to quit, as long as we're still doing it." This claim is irrefutable.

APPENDIX A: THE INTERVIEWS

Pam Hayden and Sally Dwyer-McNulty gave me a great deal of help as I tried to understand Oak Grove Church, the Philadelphia Mennonite Fellowship, and the Philadelphia Church of Christ. Hayden conducted twelve structured interviews with women from Oak Grove. Dwyer-McNulty conducted twelve similar interviews with women from the Philadelphia Mennonite Fellowship and twelve more with women from the Philadelphia Church of Christ.

Both scholars had been raised as Catholics, and neither had ever been a member of any Protestant church. Although both knew a lot about the history of religion in the United States, neither had any *particular* interest or expertise in the history of U.S. Protestantism.[1]

All the interviews Hayden and Dwyer-McNulty conducted were shaped by questionnaires that I had devised with the help of scholars at the University of Chicago and at Princeton University. Hayden and Dwyer-McNulty made audiotapes of each interview and also wrote fairly detailed fieldnotes for each one.

Both Hayden and Dwyer-McNulty conducted the interviews with considerable tact and great diplomacy, trying to avoid questions that would have caused pain or embarrassment. They skated around some issues that were too touchy for the women to talk about directly.

Hayden and Dwyer-McNulty were treated well by the women they interviewed. Indeed, in the course of the interviews, the women from the three churches seemed to have grown quite fond of the two scholars. Dwyer-McNulty was able to write in a note about one of her last interviews: "[Margaret Drake] was happy to see me. She has really come out of her shell. I think she likes the opportunity to talk about herself and what she thinks is important. I'm glad she's come to enjoy our conversations." At least one of the women—Eleanor Gregory, from the Philadelphia Mennonite Fellowship—seemed to have viewed the interviews as a chance to offer some kindly instructions concerning how to live a good life. Gregory told Dwyer-McNulty "that she thought of these interviews as mentoring. She was the older woman talking to the younger woman about life."[2]

APPENDIX B: MONEY MATTERS

The following presents the financial dimensions of the three congregations during the period of my fieldwork in as much detail as I was able to obtain.

OAK GROVE CHURCH

During the fall of 1992, Anthony Broyles, one of my research assistants, attended services at Oak Grove Church. He was given a pamphlet, "Annual Church Report," that covered the period between September 1, 1991, and August 31, 1992. Although the budget of the Oak Grove Christian Academy was kept distinct from that of the church itself, there was no fire wall between the two.[1] Money problems at the academy could also mean money problems for the church, whose leaders were seeing what could be done about the gap between the academy's income and its expenses.

During the year in question, the academy's income was $1,574,984, most ($1,273,543) from tuition. Total expenses were $1,663,850, most ($1,245,879) for salary and benefits. The budget of the church itself was not as large as that of the academy. Nevertheless, it could hardly be described as small. The church's total expenditures during the year were $393,750, including $158,310 for salaries and benefits, $50,816 for utilities, $49,413 for operating expenses, $19,070 for maintenance and repairs, and $16,552 to underwrite a "bus ministry." The church's total receipts for the period were $396,914, or $7,632.96 per week. Attendance at the Sunday morning services averaged 293.[2] So $26.05 is a rough measure of how much each person who attended Oak Grove on any given Sunday would have had to give to the church for receipts to reach that total.

Most of what I know about Oak Grove I know from participation in worship services and from talking to people I met there, who did not talk much about their annual incomes or their total assets. At Oak Grove, as at many other places, it would have been considered rude for anyone to talk too directly about such matters. Although I tried with some regularity to steer conversations toward these topics (and toward topics that would shed some indirect light on them), I did not have much luck doing so. Therefore, I know less about the finances of the people in Oak Grove than I do about those of Oak Grove itself. I have very little hard data on how much money the people made a year or had accumulated in their lives. The data I do have are presented below.

From time to time, I thought that some of the members of Oak Grove might have a higher income than I did. (I did not get this impression at either of the other churches.) A number of the people struck as me the sort who ran small but profitable businesses. I also met some people who seemed to be making a decent living in one of the professions. I ran into several schoolteachers, and I also heard that doctors and lawyers were associated with the church or the academy.

Some of the people lived in quite prosperous neighborhoods. One of the women Hayden interviewed, for example, lived in an area where the median household income was $62,635 (see Table 2, Appendix C), quite high by Philadelphia standards. The 1989 median household income for the Philadelphia Metropolitan Statistical Area as a whole was $34,400.[3] The leadership of Oak Grove Church came from the business classes, so you might not be surprised to learn that some people lived in prosperous neighborhoods. But I want to note, and emphasize, that they were only a minority.

The other woman Hayden interviewed lived in an area where the median household income was $33,041, slightly below the figure for the Philadelphia Metropolitan Statistical Area as a whole. The people who lived in the immediate vicinity of the church building—there were quite a few—were in an even less prosperous area. As Table 2 shows, the 1989 median household income in the area that contains the building in which the Oak Grove congregation met for worship was only $25,553.

I also want to stress that many—most, I would think—of the members of the church came from the working class, as shown by the ways in which they dressed, talked, and decorated their houses. Thomas Stuart's "Fundamentalism, American Capitalism, and Culture" reinforces that impression. It asserts that the fathers in most of the families in Oak Grove made their living as "working-class laborers." For many years the church had been unable to "attract and keep college graduates," and many of the children who attended Oak Grove Academy came from blue-collar homes. Their fathers worked as maintenance men, mechanics, firefighters, police officers, and lathe workers.[4]

Because of the state of Philadelphia's economy, unemployment—or the fear of unemployment—figured quite prominently. Quite early in my fieldwork, I was struck by how often these issues figured in prayers, prayer requests, and sermons.[5] Indeed, the men of Oak Grove were told from time to time that the precariousness of their economic situations was one of the reasons they needed to fix their hopes on Jesus Christ.[6] According to one of the men, Oak Grove Christian Academy's financial troubles were due, at least in part, to the fact that the parents of some of its students were losing their jobs and so were unable to pay the tuition bills. The same man told me that the church's financial troubles were also partly due to the fact that a number of its members had lost their jobs and were thus unable to make generous contributions to the congregation.

CHURCH OF CHRIST

The first time I attended a meeting at the Philadelphia Church of Christ, on October 9, 1991, I was given a pamphlet—"Budget Presentation, Fall 1991"—on which the following is based.

The Philadelphia Church of Christ spent a lot of money during the first nine months of 1991—$466,523. Of those expenditures, 43 percent were for personnel; 34 percent for missions; 12 percent for renting facilities and equipment; and the rest for such items as travel, administration, lodging, meals, special events, and so on. During those first nine months, the church received $251,331 earmarked for missions and $236,336 in contributions that were not earmarked, a total of $487,667. This works out to $12,504 a week for the nine-month period.

The Philadelphia Church of Christ was not tiny, nor was it one of the larger congregations in the United States. During the first nine months of 1991, membership never exceeded 260. At times, it was as low as 210.[7] It is possible that a large proportion of the contributions to the congregation came from people who were not members, although I encountered nothing that led me to believe that that was the case. But for the sake of argument, let's say that 10 percent of those contributions ($1,250 per week) came from people who were not members of the congregation. Dividing the remaining $11,254 by 260 gives $43, roughly what each of the 260 members would have to contribute to the church *each week* to account for the contributions it actually received. As anyone who has ever played even a minor role in drawing up a budget for a voluntary association knows, that is an impressive figure. Not many voluntary associations of any sort in Philadelphia could truthfully claim that their members make such high weekly contributions.[8]

How could so much money come from so few people? One possible explanation is that there were a few people in the congregation who were quite rich, all of whom give thousands of dollars to the congregation each month. I saw nothing to make me think that explanation is the correct one, but I saw a lot of things to support another explanation: that many of the members give a lot to the church in spite of the fact that they don't make a huge amount of money. One of the sheets in "Budget Presentation, Fall 1991"also supports this explanation. It reports the results of a survey the church conducted in January 1991 of 125 members. As you would expect, the report is not characterized by scientific rigor. The figures it gives are not, for instance, labeled as means, medians, or averages. Still, the document is a highly interesting one.

The income a typical member took home each month was $1,227. The typical member paid $331 for rent or housing. The "regular contribution" a typical member had given in the previous week was $41.[9] So, in those months with four weeks, contributions would equal $164. In the months with five weeks, the total would be $205. That would mean that in those months with four weeks' worth of contributions, a typical member would have only $732 to cover *all expenses other than housing and church contributions.* In months with five weeks, the total would, of course, be lower yet—$691. For a good proportion of the congregation, that was not enough money to make ends meet. The report suggests that a typical member had run up a credit card debt of $1,841, with other debts of $6,993. Half of the people who responded to the questionnaire said that they were behind on at least some bill payments. Almost as many said that they had bounced checks in the last year.

These figures imply the following answer to the question about how so much money could come from so few people: *many people whose economic situations were marginal—perhaps even precarious—decided that they were not going to let their lack of financial security keep them from giving lots of money to the Philadelphia Church of Christ*. I am comfortable with this answer. It coincides well with a great deal of what I saw and heard, although it is almost certainly not the whole story. And there is another aspect that I want to emphasize.

Although the congregation included many people whose economic situations were quite marginal, it also included some who were not poor and a few who were quite well off. One of the women Dwyer-McNulty interviewed said that many of the members of the congregation who lived in the city's western suburbs were part of what she thought of as the movement's "beautiful set." I could not tell exactly what that term meant, but it seemed that the people in the beautiful set had at least these characteristics: they had been with the movement throughout a good portion of its history; they were over the age of 30; they were bright and energetic; *they were not poor*.

These neighborhoods included many households that were not poor. Table 2 shows the 1989 median household income for these areas. One of the women lived in an area where the median household income was $47,318, the other where it was $38,825. Those figures are by many measures fairly high.[10] And it is also clear that the people at the church believed that a *sizable* minority of the families in the congregation had incomes that were fairly high. One member told me, for example, that about 10 or 15 percent of the families had incomes of over $60,000.[11]

So, by the time I had concluded my fieldwork at the Philadelphia Church of Christ, I had come to believe that the church had a number of members whose economic situation was quite marginal *and* that it also included some people who might be classified as comfortable or even well off. Some of the members were—to paraphrase an observation made during the first meeting I attended at the church—no longer people of want.[12]

MENNONITE FELLOWSHIP

When I first attended a meeting at the Philadelphia Mennonite Fellowship on January 12, 1992, I was given several handouts about the church's proposed budget for that year. At that time, 102 adults were either "members" of or "regular attenders" at the fellowship.[13] The budgeted expenditures were far smaller than the budgets of the two other churches. The proposed annual budget for 1992 was $73,933. It allocated $49,372 for "administration," mostly for the minister's salary and benefits. It also set aside $14,586 for "property," mostly for the rent for the building in which the church met on Sundays. The rest of the budget, $9,975, was divided into three categories: program, local ministries, and churchwide ministries. These categories included such expenses as a mutual aid fund ($1,300), a contribution to the Franconia Mennonite Conference ($2,000), and the purchase of advertisements for the church ($400).

When the handouts were being prepared, the church had not had time to come up with an absolutely accurate, final accounting of the amount of money it had been given in 1991. Its best estimate for that figure was $63,600.

The proposed budget for 1992 estimated that the church would receive a total of $66,583 in contributions during 1992,[14] or $1,280 a week. Dividing $1,280 by 102 yields $13, some idea of how much each of the 102 adults who were either members or regular attendees would have had to give weekly for the congregation to achieve its budgeted receipts.[15] That does not seem like a great deal of money to me.

Of the three churches in which I did fieldwork, the members of the Philadelphia Mennonite Fellowship seemed to have the most cultural capital. One might think that people with a lot of cultural capital would also be quite well off financially. One might think that they would be in a position to make generous contributions to their church. Why didn't that occur?

One possible explanation is that although the people were quite rich, they chose not to give their money to the church. I don't think that was true.

Another possible explanation is that the people chose not to give quite so sacrificially as did the members of the Church of Christ. There is probably some truth to that explanation. The Mennonites would have been uncomfortable with the exhortations to give lots and lots and more and more that I heard frequently at the Church of Christ. Indeed, they might not have allowed them. Taking an offering was never a part of the service at the fellowship.

Another possible explanation would run as follows: although many of the people had cultural capital, most of them failed to earn as much money as they could have if they had paid more attention to "economic reason."[16] Embracing an ideology that glorified "voluntary simplicity," they made choices that produced relatively low incomes and thus had less money at their disposal than one might have first imagined.

A good deal of what I saw and heard could be fit into such an explanation. Many people seemed to have deliberately chosen forms of employment that did not pay very well. One man, for instance, worked for a Christian school rather than a public one. Another member—a man with a degree from Harvard Law School—worked for the legal aid society rather than for a law firm that could have paid him much more. Another member—an unusually intelligent woman with a degree from Dartmouth College—left her job in the insurance industry and began working for a Christian magazine after her conversion to Christianity.

Few of the Mennonites spent a lot of money on memberships in gyms, on clothes, or on cars, and few of them lived in prestigious neighborhoods. Many lived in the immediate vicinity of the building in which the fellowship met for worship each Sunday. These neighborhoods could not be described in prosperous. As Table 2 shows, the 1989 median household income in that area was $22,617.

Neither of the members of the congregation that Dwyer-McNulty interviewed lived near that building. Both of them lived in the part of Philadelphia called Germantown. As Table 2 shows, the 1989 median household income for the areas in which those women lived was not very high—$23,269 and $18,394.[17]

So, to return to a question I asked earlier, why did the Philadelphia Mennonite Fellowship receive fairly modest contributions from the congregation? First, the church chose not to put a lot of overt pressure on people to make sacrificial contributions. In that respect, it contrasts sharply with the Philadelphia Church of Christ. Second, many of the people had less money at their disposal than one might have first imagined.

APPENDIX C: TABLES

TABLE I. 1989 MEDIAN HOUSEHOLD INCOMES IN TWO SELECTED AREAS OF PHILADELPHIA

Block group of which the 200 block of South Nineteenth Street is a part	37,431
Philadelphia Metropolitan Statistical Area	34,400
Block group of which the 800 block of South Nineteenth Street is a part	7,389

Source: U.S. Census, 1990.

TABLE 2. 1989 MEDIAN HOUSEHOLD INCOMES IN
ZIP CODE AREAS OF THE THREE CHURCHES

Area (zip code)	Median Household Income
Oak Grove Church[a]	
One (19422)	$62,635
Two (19115)	$33,041
Three (19120)	$25,553
Philadelphia Church of Christ[b]	
One (19008)	$47,318
Two (19026)	$38,825
Three (19103)	$30,718
Philadelphia Mennonite Fellowship[c]	
One (19144)	$23,269
Two (19139)	$18,394
Three (19143)	$22,617

Source: U.S. Census, 1990.

[a]Areas one and two include the houses of the two women
Hayden interviewed. Area three includes the building in which
the congregation met while I was doing my fieldwork.
[b]Areas one and two include the houses of the two women
Dwyer-McNulty interviewed. Area three includes a church
building in Center City Philadelphia in which the congregation
often met.
[c]Areas one and two include the houses of the two women
Dwyer-McNulty interviewed. Area three includes the building
in which the congregation met while I was doing my fieldwork.

NOTES

ACKNOWLEDGMENTS

1. I have assigned ficticious names to these three churches.

2. These names, as well as the names of all the other members of the three churches that appear in this book, are pseudonyms.

CHAPTER 1

1. Cf. Harding, "Convicted by the Holy Spirit"; Sinha, "Religion in an Affluent Society"; Thomas, *Doing Critical Ethnography*; and Visweswaran, *Fictions of Feminist Ethnography*.

2. Cf. Veyne, *Writing History*, 13.

3. An analysis of this pamphlet can be found in Watt, *A Transforming Faith*, 15–32.

CHAPTER 2

1. This section of the book is a pastiche. I hope that it gives a sense of what it was like to live in the city in which Oak Grove Church, the Philadelphia Mennonite Fellowship, and the Philadelphia Church of Christ are located. It is based on experiences I had while living in Philadelphia; on Kestenbaum's *Regional Almanac 1994*; on *Philadelphia,* which was written by Adams, Bartlet, Elesh, Goldstein, Kleniewski, and Yancy and published by Temple University Press in 1991; and on a set of thirteen scrapbooks I compiled during fieldwork. Most of the clippings came from Philadelphia's two largest daily newspapers, the *Daily News* and the *Inquirer.* Some of them, however, came from newspapers that were published in other cities or that presented themselves as "alternative" (in the sense of the *Village Voice* and *L.A. Weekly*). Other clippings came from newspapers that were read mostly by African Americans or by gay men and lesbians.

2. On April 1, 1996, a corporation got lots of publicity for its products through a carefully orchestrated advertising campaign announcing that it was buying the Liberty Bell. The mayor of Philadelphia told reporters that he thought the hoax was terribly clever and awfully amusing. He also told them that he was approaching the company that ran the campaign to see if it wanted to become an official corporate sponsor of the park in which the Liberty Bell is situated. When I first heard the

mayor's remarks, I hoped that he might be trying to make a joke. He wasn't, of course; he was dead serious.

3. In the summer of 1993 a man who lived in North Philadelphia known both as Earl Gant and as Abdul Rashid was arrested and charged in connection with the bombing of the World Trade Center in New York.

4. Terry Gilliam—a film director who spent some time in Philadelphia in the mid-1990s while making *Twelve Monkeys*—had a similar reaction to the city: "It's like a bull's-eye: the white suburbs, out there where the money is, then the black start of the city; then you go into Center City, which is white again, and all about money and business; then you go to City Hall and all the civil servants are black; then you go the mayor's office and he's white" (Fuchs, "The Monkeys Man," 18).

5. As Table 1 (Appendix C) indicates, the median household income in the area in which the 200 block of South Nineteenth Street is located was $37,431 in 1989.

6. On some days, one couldn't walk half a block without seeing crack vials.

7. The abandoned buildings near Nineteenth and Christian looked, and were, dangerous. While I was writing the first draft of this book (on the morning of December 30, 1995), something terrible happened to a man named Henry Wilkerson, who was sleeping in one such building at Seventeenth and Carpenter. Someone found Wilkerson that morning and doused him with an inflammable liquid, which they set on fire. Wilkerson was 61 years old when he died.

8. As Table 1 indicates, the median household income in the area in which the 800 block of South Nineteenth Street is located was $7,389 in 1989.

9. According to a study conducted by researchers at the University of Michigan, which was publicized in the Philadelphia papers, only nine cities in the United States were more segregated than Philadelphia was.

10. Eastwick, in the southwestern corner of the city, was one such neighborhood; Mt. Airy, several miles to the west and north of City Hall, was another.

11. Many of the Hispanics in Philadelphia lived in North Philadelphia; few of them lived in South Philadelphia or in the Northeast. They were very largely cut off from the rest of the city. An Anglo like me could go for days in Philadelphia without once hearing Spanish spoken on the streets of his neighborhood or in the stores downtown.

12. In the decade before I began my fieldwork, 1 percent of the households in the United States possessed 36 percent of the nation's net worth.

13. The city has been losing population for decades, too. In 1950, its population was 3,187,121; in 1992, it was 1,552,572.

14. A population survey of the Philadelphia region in the late 1980s found that 23 percent of white males, 42 percent of white females, 54 percent of black males, and 58 percent of black females were not in the work force.

15. Many of the jobs that could still be found in the region involved working for the state. Over 50,000 of the people employed in the greater Philadelphia area worked for the federal government. (The federal government was the single largest employer in the region.) Over 30,000 people worked for the Philadelphia School

District, and about the same number worked for the City of Philadelphia. The public transportation system employed about 7,000 people. About 4,000 worked for the Commonwealth of Pennsylvania. About 10,000 worked for Temple University, a commonwealth-related university that was subsidized by the Commonwealth of Pennsylvania.

16. On March 22, 1993, a *Daily News* article noted that in the previous year Philadelphia's elected representatives to the Commonwealth of Pennsylvania received $1.3 million in contributions from political action committees. Vincent Fumo, one of the most powerful politicians in Philadelphia, had garnered $195,000 all by himself. The story, which was not much different from a number of other stories in the local newspapers in the early 1990s, said that the money reflected the efforts of groups in the commonwealth to buy access to and influence over Pennsylvania's legislators.

17. While I was doing my fieldwork, it sometimes seemed as though Philadelphia—indeed, the entire United States—was a laboratory in which mad scientists were experimenting. What would happen, they wanted to know, if we let everything—including, say, education, cultural production, art, and religion—be ruled by the profit motive.

18. "Board Discussion with the President." *Temple Times*, 21 October 1994.

CHAPTER 3

1. Quoted in Davies, "Still Pooling Their Efforts," 5.

2. *Asymmetric* and *symmetric* are both complicated words. Symmetric power relations might be thought of as those relations that are pleasing to the eye, harmonious, and balanced. The phrase also suggests relations in which power flows back and forth rather than always running in a single direction. In that respect, symmetrical power relations might be regarded as the opposite of the relationship between a master and slave.

3. Boswell, *Same-Sex Unions in Premodern Europe*, 262.

4. Patton, *Sex and Germs*, 97.

5. Lowe, *The Body in Late-Capitalist USA*, 145.

6. Cohen and Arato, *Civil Society and Political Theory*, 24.

7. McGrath, "A Better Way," 311.

8. Balmer, *Mine Eyes Have Seen the Glory*, 159.

9. Tomaskovic-Devey, "The Protestant Ethic," 154.

10. Eagleton, *Ideology: An Introduction*, xi.

11. Lukacs, *The End of the Twentieth Century*, 226.

12. Nash and Jeffrey, eds., *The American People*, 931.

13. A Christian theologian might say that the five allegations are expressed in "the language of prophecy" rather than in the "the language of contemplation" (cf. Gutiérrez, *On Job*).

14. And in many journalistic circles as well:

In America, no one is required to go to the Liberty Baptist Church or watch the 700 Club. But the movements that these institutions represent and promote provide the best hope for American democracy and peace, capitalist prosperity and progress. Ironically enough, it is the so-called reactionaries who offer the best prospects for continuing American leadership in the world economy in the new era of accelerating technological change. Just as the nuclear families of Western Europe unleashed the energies of the industrial revolution, so the new miracles of modern technology are created and sustained by the moral discipline and spiritual incandescence of a culture of churches and families. In families, men and women routinely make long term commitments and sacrifices that are inexplicable and indefensible within the compass of secular hedonist values. Modern society, no less than any previous civilization, rests on the accumulated moral and spiritual capital embodied in the rock of ages. (Gilder, *Men and Marriage*, 112–13)

This paragraph is worth careful consideration. It claims that a return to traditional family values and a reinvigorated American capitalism are closely connected. The latter would be impossible, it implies, without the former.

15. Analyses that depict Bible-carrying Christian groups not simply as places that enforce asymmetrical power relationships include Ammerman, *Bible Believers*; Bendroth, *Fundamentalism and Gender*; Brusco, *The Reformation of Machismo*; Griffith, *God's Daughters*; D. G. Hart, *Defending the Faith*; McDannell, *Material Christianity*; Titon, *Powerhouse for God*; R. Stephen Warner, *New Wine in Old Wineskins*. Each has made a major contribution to our understanding of Bible-carrying Christianity in the Americas.

16. Cf. Asad, *Genealogies of Religion*, and Waugh, "Fundamentalism: Harbinger of Academic Revisionism?"

17. I talked to my mother, Elise Watt, about this on February 11, 1996. She told me that on at least one occasion—and probably on many others—the pastor of an Alabama church told Aunt Tommy that the difference between "preaching a sermon" and "delivering a talk" depended on where Aunt Tommy positioned herself in the church building. If she stood behind the pulpit, she would have been preaching a sermon, which women were not allowed to do. She therefore had to find some other and less authoritative place from which to speak. Thus situated, she was only "delivering a talk."

18. On the other hand, we would *never* have allowed two men whom we knew for a fact to be having sex with each other to become members of the church. We knew what the Bible said about sodomites.

19. My mother had attended college for two years in the early 1950s. In the 1960s, she got her bachelor's and master's degrees.

20. Cf. Williams, "Base and Superstructure."

CHAPTER 4

1. Stuart was, I would guess, about 35 or so when he wrote "Fundamentalism, Americanism, and Culture."

2. During my fieldwork at Oak Grove, I encountered very few, if any, immigrants from Brazil who were dark-skinned. Claudio Gediminis (see below), for instance, was almost as pale as I am.

3. Foster asserted in one of his sermons, for example, that his studies had given him the impression that women were treated "almost" as though they were "chattel" in first-century Palestine. He said this in a way that made me think that all real followers of Jesus would find such treatment of women appalling. Such statements—which are, of course, sometimes part of an explicit anti-Judaic polemic—are found in the writings of a great many people who think of themselves as Christian feminists.

4. These observations are based on Hayden's interview with Jane Thomas.

5. These expenditures, which seem to have been kept entirely separate from the rest of the church's budget, were overseen by a group within the church called the Women's Home and Foreign Missionary Society.

6. For a classic analysis of the "cultural captivity" of the largest Protestant denomination in the United States—the Southern Baptist Convention—see Eighmy, *Churches in Cultural Captivity*.

7. Alexander and Wallis are associated with the "evangelical left"; Ellul is a Christian anarchist.

8. What I have said here does not apply to what occurred at Wednesday night prayer meetings. In those services, the members of the congregation had a great deal of say.

9. The phrase comes from a conversation with Bob DeGregorio.

10. These phrases come from a conversation with Claudio Gediminis.

11. This phrase comes from a lecture I heard at Oak Grove Academy in a high school class on the history of the United States in the twentieth century. God was pictured as providing strength for the American prisoners of war who had to endure harsh treatment at the hands of their Communist captors.

12. I didn't say the pledge that day. Doing so would have made me feel like a hypocrite and a fool. I can't recall many other occasions during my fieldwork at Oak Grove when I refused to go along with the church's routines.

13. Bruce Comens thought that the congregation was centered around "an astonishing amalgam of Christianity and American nationalism."

14. Davis, *City of Quartz*, 3–14, contains a vivid description of the role real estate developers played in shaping the history of this region of California.

15. The leader I have particularly in mind here is Foster. In another context, he also expressed considerable annoyance at government officials whose efforts to protect the natural environment seemed to him to evince a lack of respect for the rights of landowners.

16. Comens, "The Business of Belief."

17. Ibid.

18. For an overview of the relationships between commercialism and Protestantism in the history of the United States, see Zuckerman, "Holy Wars, Civil Wars."

19. It was not unusual for services at Oak Grove to discuss homosexuality. Several of the services I attended included denunciations of it as a sin.

20. It is worth noting that the voter's guides that were distributed at the service Hayden attended strongly implied that a concern for the civil rights of lesbians and gay men could not be reconciled with a Christian view of politics.

21. Although I am focusing here on the subordinate role that women played in the life of the *church*, the women were also taught that their proper role in the home was one of "service" rather than "leadership." I suspect that nearly all the people I met at Oak Grove believed that men ought to be, as one of the men at Oak Grove told me, "the head of the house."

22. Women could, however, participate in the part of the service in which the congregation *collectively* read aloud a passage from the Bible.

23. This paragraph comes from Hayden's field notes.

CHAPTER 5

1. Watt, "Evangelicalism, the Market, and the State," 2.

2. Earlier in the week, Ed Rendell had been inaugurated as mayor. His predecessor, Wilson Goode, was mayor when the city dropped a bomb on the MOVE house. Goode's predecessor was Frank Rizzo. At one point in the service, a man prayed that the city's new leaders would prove themselves to be compassionate people. That was not said, however, in a way that *unambivalently* claimed that the city's old leaders had proved themselves to be heartless.

3. The church began asking its members to make financial pledges at the end of 1991. During my fieldwork, a fair proportion of the congregation did not do so.

4. In 1991, Temple University paid me $53,557.74.

5. The members of Congress who attended the hearing were told: "Spiritual values are real; they are not to be treated as incidental or expendable to fit the needs of the state."

6. I accepted their invitation. I was never invited to share the Lord's Supper at Oak Grove. The people at the Philadelphia Church of Christ also invited me to take communion with them, and I did so.

7. It is worth noting, I think, that some members of this congregation thought that proselytizing among some groups—among Jews, for example—might not be completely appropriate, and some non-Christians should perhaps be seen as fellow travelers rather than as potential converts. The people at the fellowship were not, however, opposed to proselytizing. They invited people to Billy Graham crusades and took great satisfaction in hearing stories about Muslims who had been converted to Christianity.

8. One of the books that the leaders of the fellowship suggested I read—Paul Lederach's *A Third Way*—makes an interesting claim about the Christian traditions that the fellowship prized most highly. In the Anabaptist/Mennonite theological heritage, it asserts, one starts to make sense of the Bible by focusing on "Jesus as he is portrayed in the Gospels" (p. 19). Lederach's book includes a chapter entitled "The Primacy of God's Kingdom."

9. Cadorette et al., *Liberation Theology*, 107.

10. Richardson and Bowden, *Westminster Dictionary*, 317.

11. Myers, *Binding the Strong Man*, 387–88. Although Myers notes the differences between Jesus and the bandits with whom he was crucified, he also argues forcefully that Jesus had more in common with them than he did with the officers of the empire who were in charge of deciding who would and who would not be crucified.

12. Here I am quoting from a hymn—"We Are People of God's Peace"—whose text is attributed to Menno Simons. The hymn can be found in *Hymnal: A Worship Book,* which was used by the fellowship during its Sunday morning services. (The book was published in 1992 by three publishers: Brethren Press, Faith and Life Press, and the Mennonite Publishing House.)

13. It would be difficult to overestimate the importance of these issues in the day-to-day life of the people. They wanted to think of themselves as peace-loving people, which was central to their understanding of themselves. But they mostly lived, worked, and worshiped in violent neighborhoods in a violent city. Philadelphia must often have seemed to them to have more in common with the violence-filled kingdoms of ancient Rome, Greece, Babylon, and Egypt than it did with the peaceful kingdom of God for which they longed.

14. This paragraph is based on a sermon David Geist preached on February 23, 1992. The sermon took the form of an explication of the Sermon on the Plain.

15. This text can be found under "worship resources" in *Hymnal.* It is assigned number 711. The line breaks and the italics in the original have been ignored in the version reproduced here.

16. The service I am referring to took place on May 3, 1992, just after the jury's decision in the first trial of the officers who had beaten Rodney King.

17. Myers, *Binding the Strong Man*, 454–57.

18. Comens, "Belief in Community."

19. Ibid.

20. The quotation comes from a conversation between Eleanor Gregory and Dwyer-McNulty.

21. The phrase comes from a conversation between Margaret Drake and Dwyer-McNulty.

22. It is possible that there was some connection between the Mennonites' suspicion of hierarchy and the postures they used in their worship services. The congregation did not bow or kneel at *any* of the services I attended. Perhaps they feared that such postures might confuse the recognition of the lordship of God with a deference to clergy.

23. The phrase comes from a conversation between Margaret Drake and Dwyer-McNulty.

24. The phrase comes from a conversation between Drake and Dwyer-McNulty.

25. My understanding of what occurred in business meetings is largely drawn from Dwyer-McNulty's conversations with Eleanor Gregory.

26. Bruce Comens's "Belief in Community" includes a comment about the congregation's skeptical appraisal of partisan politics: "I'm not sure of specific stands, but my general sense was that they were committed to a politics far more radical than the American electoral process incorporates."

27. This text is taken from "worship resources," number 803 in *Hymnal*. In the interests of readability, it is presented here without some of the typographical features (e.g., italics and boldface) of the original.

28. I was not present at this service. My account of it is based on fieldnotes by Dwyer-McNulty.

29. This illegitimacy of such an expectation is one of the major themes of Myers's *Binding the Strong Man*.

30. The phrase I have quoted was used by a young Mennonite in a discussion in a Sunday School class. He was talking about whether it was proper for Christians to turn to gun-carrying police officers for help.

31. This is not to say that American Mennonites have always and everywhere tried to maintain such a distance. Good discussions of their ambivalent attitudes toward the state can be found in Juhnke, *Vision, Doctrine, War,* 208–42; MacMaster, *Land, Piety, Peoplehood,* 229–80; Miller, *Wise as Serpents, Innocent as Doves*; Redekop, *Mennonite Society,* 215–32; and Schlabach, *Peace, Faith, Nation,* 141–200.

32. These sentiments were expressed in some comments on the sermon Geist preached on "Peace Sunday" in July 1992.

33. Cf. Redekop, *Mennonite Society,* 219.

34. My understanding of Gregory's attitudes toward the state are based on her conversations with Dwyer-McNulty. For a provocative analysis of contemporary protests against the de-Christianization of the United States, see Hollinger, *Science, Jews, and Secular Culture,* 17–41.

35. The quotations are from a conversation between Eleanor Gregory and Dwyer-McNulty.

36. These phrases are from a conversation between Margaret Drake and Dwyer-McNulty.

37. This idea is from a conversation between Gregory and Dwyer-McNulty.

38. Drake expressed this sentiment to Dwyer-McNulty.

39. Ibid.

40. This point was made quite forcefully in a set of prayers during the course of the worship service at the fellowship on February 23, 1992.

41. Drake expressed this sentiment to Dwyer-McNulty.

42. This quotation is from Dwyer-McNulty.

43. Gregory and Drake, for instance, lived in a neighborhood with many crack houses.

44. This observation is based on one of Dwyer-McNulty's conversations with Drake.

45. My source for this is a private conversation with one of the members of the congregation. I cannot say more without violating a confidence.

46. Although there is obviously nothing odd about a household in Philadelphia having to depend on wages to make ends meet, one could plausibly argue that there have been many times and places in U.S. history in which Bible-carrying Christians have not been as dependent on income from wages as were the Mennonites. Good discussions of this issue can be found in Zuckerman's "Holy Wars," Titon's *Powerhouse for God*, and Fields's "Understanding Activist Fundamentalism." Smith and Wallerstein, eds., *Creating and Transforming Households*, contains an extremely helpful analysis of the way in which households work in the modern world.

47. This observation is based on a conversation between Margaret Drake and Dwyer-McNulty.

48. Some of the reasons that one might see devotion to the family as unbiblical are discussed, in a somewhat polemical fashion, in Boswell, *Same-Sex Unions in Premodern Europe*, and in Mount, *The Subversive Family*, 15–28. The scholarly literature on religion in the United States suggests that there was nothing especially atypical about the fellowship's attachment to the family, which has been a defining characteristic of many twentieth-century Christian communities in the United States. See, for example, Orsi, *The Madonna of 115th Street*, and Warner, *New Wine in Old Wineskins*.

49. The quotations in this sentence are from Dwyer-McNulty's interviews with Drake.

50. The part of the worship service devoted to sharing joys and concerns was not thought of as a supplement to the "real" heart of the service but rather as a crucial part.

51. This paragraph and the two that follow are based largely on Dwyer-McNulty's conversations with Gregory and Drake. It is possible that the range of opinion to be found at the fellowship on sex outside of marriage was actually somewhat wider than those conversations and these paragraphs indicate.

52. This story, which concerns the experiences of two Sunday School teachers who were living together without being married, is based on Dwyer-McNulty's interviews with Gregory.

53. The booklet *Christians and Homosexuality*, which was written by Bible-carrying Christians, displays a good deal of tolerance for homosexuality. Indeed, at some points the booklet goes beyond mere tolerance. For a helpful study of gay people in religious organizations in the contemporary United States, see Comstock, *Unrepentant, Self-Affirming, Practicing*.

54. This phrase is from Dwyer-McNulty's interviews with Gregory.

55. This phrase is from Dwyer-McNulty's interviews with Drake.

56. I am grateful to Robert Orsi for helping me to see this point.

57. This sentence and the two that precede it are based on Dwyer-McNulty's conversations with Gregory.

58. During the Sunday morning worship service on July 26, 1992, I jotted down the following note: "The preacher is a woman. The moderator is a woman. The song leader is a woman. When someone in the congregation speaks, at least today, that person is more likely to be a woman than a man."

59. In November 1992, Geist gave a presentation to one of my classes at Temple. A student asked: "What can't women do in your church?" Geist responded: "Be silent."

60. This analysis of equality and complementarity surfaced in Gregory's conversations with Dwyer-McNulty.

61. It is possible that the attitudes that Gregory and Drake expressed to Dwyer-McNulty about how women should be treated in the home and in the workplace were somewhat more "traditional" than the attitudes that many other members of the congregation would have expressed in a similar setting.

62. This became clear in the course of Gregory's conversations with Dwyer-McNulty. There were, however, limits to this submission. Gregory made it clear, for example, that she did not have a duty to have sex with her husband whenever he wanted to have sex with her.

63. It should probably also be noted that both Gregory and Drake held to convictions about the proper role of women in Christian churches that were not especially liberal. Drake told Dwyer-McNulty that she thought that "women made better counselors than ministers." Gregory told Dwyer-McNulty that she was still getting used to the idea of women taking positions of leadership in the church and that she was not sure that she would encourage her daughter to consider becoming a minister of the gospel. (Sons would, I gathered, have been a different story.)

CHAPTER 6

1. Donald E. Miller, *Reinventing American Protestantism.*

2. For a helpful account of this movement, which places it firmly in the context of the history of the Church of Christ, see Hughes, *Reviving the Ancient Faith*, 359–63.

3. Giambarba, *Bent on Conquest*, v.

4. Kip McKean, "Revolution Through Restoratation."

5. As you might guess, there are relatively few congregations in southeastern Pennsylvania that are racially integrated.

6. According to one of the speakers, the average member of the congregation was giving the church about $25 per week. Each person needed to raise his or her weekly donation by $4 per week.

7. By mixed assemblies, I mean meetings that were attended by both women and men.

8. I did talk to a representative of the dean of students. The conversation, however, did not do the Philadelphia Church of Christ any good.

9. I did talk to the reporter. Our conversation did not have much if any influence on what she told her viewers about the church.

10. I never really got the hang of the hand clapping. I always felt clumsy—a middle-class, white guy trying to pretend that he wasn't middle class and white.

11. During our basketball games, I did end up using such language. My doing so caused me and the other men in the game a good deal of embarrassment.

12. When I slipped—for example, using the word *aesthetics* while watching a baseball game—I felt silly.

13. I also tried, however, to dress slightly more formally at the Church of Christ than I would have for worship services at my home congregations. At the Church of Christ, people sometimes seemed to be "dressing for success."

14. Cf. Sinha, "Religion in an Affluent Society."

15. A particularly provocative example of this argument can be found in R. Stephen Warner's "Work in Progress Toward a New Paradigm for the Sociological Study of Religion in the United States." Warner argues, for instance, that religion has greatly empowered homosexuals in the United States. He does not devote much attention to those aspects of the history of religion that don't support that claim.

16. For an ethnographic gloss on the tensions between religious commitment and some features of contemporary U.S. society, see Liebow, *Tell Them Who I Am*, 177.

17. It is not hard for me to believe that her claim was true. Professors at the colleges and universities where I studied said similar things.

18. See Schwartz, *The Curse of Cain*, for a provocative discussion of the role of violence in the Hebrew Bible.

19. The Great Commission runs as follows: "Then Jesus came to them and said, 'All authority in heaven and on earth has been given to me. Therefore go and make disciples of all nations, baptizing them in the name of the Father and of the Son and of the Holy Spirit, and teaching them to obey everything I have commanded you. And surely I will be with you always, to the very end of the age'" (Matthew 28.18–20, NRSV). For an excellent analysis of the anti-Judaic elements in Christian Scriptures, see Daniel Boyarin's *A Radical Jew*. I don't mean to imply that the monotheistic religions are the only cultural formations both empowering and prone to creating asymmetric power relations. A similar argument could be made, I'm sure, about voodoo (Brown, *Mama Lola*), about many other cultural formations that are usually labeled religious (Bloch, *Prey into Hunter*), and about psychoanalysis (Steedman, *Landscape for a Good Woman*). But it might be true that Christianity, Judaism, Islam, and other monotheistic traditions are both particularly empowering and particularly congruent with asymmetric power relations. The views of Gordon Kaufman, the noted Christian theologian, are worth considering on this point: "It is precisely because monotheism is totalitarian—that is, has implications for all dimensions of life, including what we might otherwise think of as secular domains—that it can have great unifying power and meaning; but, as we have observed, this also opens it to very serious forms of corruption and abuse" (*In Face of Mystery*, 82).

20. Giambarba, *Bent on Conquest*, x.

21. According to the biblical account, the destruction of Jericho was (in some strong, if unspecified, sense) a direct consequence of God's leading the Israelites out of the land where they had been enslaved.

22. The way in which the ministers exercised their authority in public meetings gave the men who spoke a lot of opportunities to tease their wives. Since the church did not believe that it was proper for a woman to speak in a public meeting at which men were present, I never heard a joke that went the other way. Sometimes the jokes that husbands made about their wives seemed clever and affectionate. Most of the time they didn't. The way in which ministerial authority was exercised at the church also gave whites a lot of opportunities to tease blacks and to tease black culture. These opportunities were exploited with some avidity, but the jokes never stuck me as overtly racist. Indeed, the men who made them were—so a number of black people told me—entirely free of racial prejudice. However, the jokes almost always went one way. In the public meetings, whites kidded blacks a lot more often than blacks kidded whites. In the interest of fairness, I ought to point out that on at least one occasion, I heard a minister warn in one of the services that what he was about to say might be incorrect and that it was *not* an official teaching. He emphasized that he was speaking as an "individual," not as a spokesman for the church. However, that sort of remark was not made with any frequency in the services of the Church of Christ.

23. Baird, "A New Look at Authority," 18.

24. Castelli's *Imitating Paul* includes a helpful discussion of this issue.

25. For influential and interesting reflections on the meaning of conversion in a group with some similarities to the Church of Christ, see Harding, "Convicted by the Holy Spirit." For superb studies of the relationship between conversion and the globalization of Christianity, see Comaroff and Comaroff, *Of Revelation and Revolution*, and the articles in Veer, *Conversion to Modernities*.

26. In doing so, I probably overstepped my bounds. The next day I apologized for being overly judgmental.

27. The New International Version, the translation that Calvert was using while we spoke.

28. For an influential analysis of medieval Christian techniques that bear a strong resemblance to those I encountered at the Church of Christ, see Asad, *Genealogies of Religion*, 83–168.

29. Hill, *The English Bible and the Seventeenth-Century Revolution*, presents a useful analysis of some of the difficulties involved in trying to resolve disagreements by appealing to biblical authority.

30. Cf. Gorz, *Critique of Economic Reason*.

31. Emma Roberts told Dwyer-McNulty that she knew that she and her husband would have a higher standard of living if they gave less money to the church. There was, she said, a part of her that regretted not being able to afford some of the things other members of her extended family could afford. All in all, though, she was comfortable with the decision she and her husband had made.

32. The quote is from Roberts.

33. Giambarba, *Bent on Conquest*, 42.

34. It would be possible to argue that the Church of Christ was itself an arm of the entertainment industry. Admission was charged for a number of the events—concerts and picnics, for instance—that the church used to attract new members. Religious magazines, books on child rearing, guides for winning other people to Christ, and hymnals were sold at many worship services sponsored by the church.

35. Later in the interview, Roberts expressed a more ambivalent attitude about some of the things that people fighting for their country sometimes have to do.

36. In the course of a presentation he was making to one of my classes, Doug Jensen, a leader in the Church of Christ, was asked by a student how churches should teach their members about the government. Jensen said that Christians should be taught that they "need to support the state" and "respect the authorities." Christians should realize that people who occupied positions of power in the government were there because God had put them there.

37. It is interesting that Calvert himself had gotten into trouble with government authorities: his missionary activities in India eventually led to his expulsion.

38. In this paragraph I am drawing partly on notes I made after a conversation with Walter Elliot.

39. Several scholarly investigations of the practices of Bible-carrying Christian Protestants have concluded that many demonstrate relatively little interest in partisan politics. Steve Bruce, for example, argues: "Some conservative Protestants choose Pietistic retreat from the world on its own intrinsic merits as an alternative to imposing their righteousness on the unregenerate" (*Rise and Fall of the New Christian Right*, 175).

40. The phrase and the sentiment are from a talk Doug Jensen gave to one of my classes at Temple University.

41. The phrase is from Dwyer-McNulty. Participation in these rituals was almost mandatory. On certain days of the year, for example, all the single people in the church were encouraged—directed, almost—to go out on dates with other single members.

42. Eleana McKean, "Strong to Serve," 14 (emphasis added). I am not in a position to prove that McKean's claim is true.

43. Emma Roberts found this portion of the interviews particularly interesting. She was, Dwyer-McNulty noted, literally sitting on the edge of her seat as she spoke about what a good job the church did in fostering strong marriages.

44. The quotation is from Sarah Mather.

45. I am relying here on Dwyer-McNulty's interviews with Roberts.

46. Mather's feeling of being condemned reminds us of Monique Wittig's famous assertion: one cannot be born a woman—one can only become, or resist becoming, one. This makes a great deal of sense. One could say, perhaps, that one of the most important social roles of churches like the Church of Christ is this: they create social spaces in which some people are encouraged—almost forced, in fact—to become women.

47. Cf. Brusco, *The Reformation of Machismo*.

48. Cf. Liebow, *Tell Them Who I Am*, 81–114.

49. Kip McKean, "Revolution Through Restoration," includes a description of Guthrie's role in the history of the movement.

50. It was, as you might well imagine, difficult for me to learn much about the Bible-study groups and discipling partnerships run by women counselors. My desire to learn more about them is what first led me to hire women research assistants.

51. Roberts's comments to Dwyer-McNulty are what I particularly have in mind here.

52. This is a quotation from Mather.

APPENDIX A: THE INTERVIEWS

1. At the time she conducted her interviews, Hayden was in her 30s, unmarried, and the mother of two young children. Dwyer-McNulty was in her mid-20s and married. She had no children.

2. It is interesting that some of what Eleanor Gregory told Dwyer-McNulty was strictly off the record. Those remarks were neither taped nor transcribed.

APPENDIX B: MONEY MATTERS

1. I was given the impression, for example, that a good many—perhaps all—of the academy's utility bills were paid out of the church's funds.

2. These figures almost certainly included many people—for example, children and teenagers—whose financial contributions to the church were quite modest. The figures for average attendance at Oak Grove were not reliable guides to the total membership in the church. The members had considerably higher-than-average attendance. In Melton, *National Directory of Churches, Synagogues, and Other Houses of Worship*, Oak Grove's "size"—which in that volume seems to have meant something like "the number of names on the membership rolls"—was categorized as "between 501 and 2500."

3. The Philadelphia Metropolitan Statistical Area is made up of the city of Philadelphia and eight surrounding counties. Half are in Pennsylvania (Bucks, Chester, Delaware, and Montgomery) and half are in New Jersey (Burlington, Camden, Gloucester, and Salem).

4. The man who told me this was Bob DiFranco, one of the leaders of Oak Grove Academy.

5. This involved only men. I don't recall any occasions in which a story about a woman who had lost her job or worried about losing her job figured in public worship.

6. In May 1992, for example, the men were asked a rhetorical question from the pulpit: "Can you be sure that your world will last?" The answer that was supplied to them was no. "The whole company [for which you work] could be shut down tomorrow."

7. Average Sunday attendance at the Church of Christ never exceeded 400 during the first nine months of 1991. Sometimes it barely exceeded 300.

8. Although I think of myself as moderately devout and though I am (by many standards) wealthy, for only one or two years in my life have I contributed that much money to any church.

9. It is worth noting that the Philadelphia Church of Christ's report on what its members gave ($41 a week) is close but not identical to the figure my calculations produced.

10. The house of one of the members of the Philadelphia Church of Christ that I visited, in the western suburbs of the city, must have been quite expensive. My guess is that it might bring as much as $500,000 if it were sold.

11. That was, of course, an estimate. I am quite sure that the man who gave me the estimate was referring to household income rather than to individual income.

12. The man who preached that night said: "I am not now a man of want. But I have been. And I still sacrifice."

13. I was not able to determine how many of the 102 were only regular attenders and how many were actual members.

14. The proposed budget also included a $6,000 subsidy from the Franconia Conference of the Mennonite Church.

15. The budget did not have any formal category for evaluating the amount of unpaid labor that members of the congregation contributed to it, but I believe that it was considerable.

16. Gorz, *Critique of Economic Reason*.

17. In the course of one of her conversations with Dwyer-McNulty, Eleanor Gregory "thought out loud" about the neighborhood in which her family lived. She said that when she and her husband first moved, they didn't give a lot of thought to whether it was a safe neighborhood, but crime had become a problem. A car-stealing ring had started to use a part of the block as a sort of a garage to change tires and license plates on stolen cars. A good deal of drug trafficking was going on nearby.

BIBLIOGRAPHY

Abercrombie, Nicholas, and Bryan S. Turner. "The Dominant Ideology Thesis." In *Classes, Power, and Conflict: Classical and Contemporary Debates,* ed. Anthony Giddens and David Held. Berkeley: University of California Press, 1982.

Adams, Carolyn, David Bartelt, David Elesh, Ira Goldstein, Nancy Kleniewski, and William Yancy. *Philadelphia: Neighborhoods, Divisions, and Conflict in a Postindustrial City.* Philadelphia: Temple University Press, 1991.

Albanese, Catherine L. *America, Religions and Religion.* Belmont, Calif.: Wadsworth, 1992.

Ammerman, Nancy Tatom. *Bible Believers: Fundamentalists in the Modern World.* New Brunswick, N.J.: Rutgers University Press, 1987.

———. *Baptist Battles: Social Change and Religious Conflict.* New Brunswick, N.J.: Rutgers University Press, 1990

Anderson, Robert Mapes. *Vision of the Disinherited: The Making of American Pentecostalism.* New York: Oxford University Press, 1979.

Asad, Talal. *Genealogies of Religion: Discipline and Reasons of Power in Christianity and Islam.* Baltimore: Johns Hopkins University Press, 1993.

Atkinson, Paul. *Understanding Ethnographic Texts.* Newbury Park, Calif.: Sage, 1992.

Baer, Hans A., and Merrill Singer. *African-American Religion in the Twentieth Century.* Knoxville: University of Tennessee Press, 1992.

Bailyn, Bernard. *Education in the Forming of American Society.* New York: Norton, 1960.

———. "The Challenge of Modern Historiography." *American Historical Review* 87 (1982): 1–24.

Baird, Al. "A New Look at Authority." *UpsideDown,* April 1992, 17–19, 49.

Balmer, Randall. *Mine Eyes Have Seen the Glory: A Journey into the Evangelical Subculture in America.* New York: Oxford University Press, 1989.

Balmer, Randall, and Jesse T. Todd, Jr. "Calvary Chapel, Costa Mesa, California." In *American Congregations,* 2 vols., ed. James P. Wind and James W. Lewis. Chicago: University of Chicago Press, 1994.

Barron, Bruce. *The Health and Wealth Gospel: A Fresh Look at Healing, Prosperity and Positive Confession.* Downers Grove, Ill.: InterVarsity Press, 1987.

Bedell, Kenneth B., ed. *Yearbook of American and Canadian Churches, 1995.* Nashville, Tenn.: Abingdon, 1995.

Bender, Thomas. "Wholes and Parts: The Need for Synthesis in American History." *Journal of American History* 73 (1986): 120–36.

Bendroth, Margaret Lamberts. *Fundamentalism and Gender, 1875 to the Present.* New Haven, Conn.: Yale University Press, 1993.

———. "Women in Twentieth-Century Evangelicalism." *Evangelical Studies Bulletin* 13 (1996): 4–6.

Benedict of Nursia. *The Rule of Saint Benedict.* Leominster, England: Gracewing, 1990.

Billings, Dwight B. "Religion as Opposition: A Gramscian Analysis." *American Journal of Sociology* 96 (1990): 1–31.

Billings, Dwight B., and Shaunna L. Scott. "Religion and Political Legitimation." *Annual Review of Sociology* 20 (1994): 173–201.

Bizzinger, Buzz. *A Prayer for the City.* New York: Random House, 1997.

Bloch, Maurice. *Prey into Hunter: The Politics of Religious Experience.* Cambridge: Cambridge University Press, 1992.

Blumhofer, Edith L., and Joel A. Carpenter, eds. *Twentieth-Century Evangelicalism: A Guide to the Sources.* New York: Garland Press, 1990.

Boswell, John. *Same-Sex Unions in Premodern Europe.* New York: Villard Books, 1994.

Boyarin, Daniel. *A Radical Jew: Paul and the Politics of Identity.* Berkeley: University of California Press, 1994.

———. "Rabbinic Resistance to Male Domination." In *Interpreting Judaism in a Postmodern Age,* ed. Steven Kepnes. New York: New York University Press, 1996.

Brasher, Brenda. *Godly Women: Fundamentalism and Female Power.* New Brunswick, N.J.: Rutgers University Press, 1998.

Brown, Karen McCarthy. *Mama Lola: A Vodou Priestess in Brooklyn.* Berkeley: University of California Press, 1991.

Browning, Don S. "The Religion, Culture, and Family Project." *Criterion* 32 (1993): 5–11.

Bruce, Steve. *The Rise and the Fall of the New Christian Right: Conservative Protestant Politics in America, 1978–1988.* Oxford: Clarendon, 1990.

Brusco, Elizabeth E. *The Reformation of Machismo: Evangelical Conversion and Gender in Colombia.* Austin: University of Texas Press, 1995.

Cadorette, Curt, Marie Giblin, J. Marilyn Legge, and Mary Snyder, eds. *Liberation Theology: An Introductory Reader.* Maryknoll, N.Y.: Orbis, 1992.

Calhoun, Craig. "Civil Society and the Public Sphere." *Public Culture* 5 (1993): 267–80.

Calhoun, Craig, ed. *Habermas and the Public Sphere.* Cambridge, Mass.: MIT Press, 1992.

Carpenter, Joel A. "Fundamentalist Institutions and the Rise of Evangelical Protestantism, 1929–1942." *Church History* 49 (1980): 62–75.

———. "From Fundamentalism to the New Evangelical Coalition." In *Evangelicalism and Modern America*, ed. George Marsden. Grand Rapids, Mich.: Eerdmans, 1984.

———. "The Fundamentalist Leaven and the Rise of an Evangelical United Front." In *The Evangelical Tradition in America*, ed. Leonard I. Sweet, 257–88. Macon, Ga.: Mercer University Press, 1984.

———. "Revive Us Again: Alienation, Hope, and the Resurgence of Fundamentalism, 1930–1950." In *Transforming Faith: The Sacred and the Secular in Modern American History*, ed. M. L. Bradbury and James B. Gilbert, 105–25. New York: Greenwood, 1989.

Carroll, Jackson W., and Penny Long Marler. "Culture Wars? Insights from Ethnographies of Two Protestant Seminaries." *Sociology of Religion* 56 (1995): 1–20.

Castelli, Elizabeth A. *Imitating Paul: A Discourse of Power*. Louisville, Ky.: Westminster/John Knox, 1991.

Childers, Joseph, and Gary Hentzi, eds. *The Columbia Dictionary of Modern Literary and Cultural Criticism*. New York: Columbia University Press, 1995.

Chopp, Rebecca S. "Feminist Queries and Metaphysical Musings." *Modern Theology* 11 (1995): 47–63.

Christians and Homosexuality. Philadelphia: Other Side, 1994.

Churchill, Ward. *Indians Are Us? Culture and Genocide in Native North America*. Monroe, Me.: Common Courage Press, 1994.

Cohen, Jean L., and Andrew Arato. *Civil Society and Political Theory*. Cambridge, Mass.: MIT Press, 1992.

Comaroff, Jean, and John Comaroff. *Of Revelation and Revolution: Christianity, Colonialism, and Consciousness in South Africa*. Chicago: University of Chicago Press, 1991.

Comens, Bruce. "Belief in Community: A Report on a Visit to the Philadelphia Mennonite Fellowship." Unpublished manuscript, 1992.

———. "Belief Is an Attitude: A Report on Visits to the Church of Christ." Unpublished manuscript, 1992.

———. "The Business of Belief: A Report on a Visit to the Oak Grove Church." Unpublished manuscript, 1992.

Comstock, Gary David. *Unrepentant, Self-Affirming, Practicing: Lesbian/Bisexual/Gay People Within Organized Religion*. New York: Continuum, 1996.

Coontz, Stephanie. *The Social Origins of Private Life: A History of American Families, 1600–1900*. London: Verso, 1988.

———. *The Way We Never Were: American Families and the Nostalgia Trap*. New York: Basic Books, 1992.

Covington, Dennis. *Salvation on Sand Mountain: Snake Handling and Redemption in Southern Appalachia.* Reading, Mass.: Addison-Wesley, 1995.

Davies, Dave. "Still Pooling Their Efforts." *Philadelphia Daily News,* June 14, 1996, 5.

Davis, Mike. *City of Quartz: Excavating the Future in Los Angeles.* New York: Vintage Books, 1992.

Day, Katie. "The Extension of Our Dreams." Unpublished manuscript, 1995.

———. "A Place to Let My Light Shine." Unpublished manuscript, 1995.

Dayton, Donald W. "Social and Political Conservatism and Modern American Evangelicalism: A Preliminary Search for the Reasons." *Union Seminary Quarterly Review* 32 (1977): 71–80.

———. "Yet Another Layer of the Onion: Or Opening the Ecumenical Door to Let the Riffraff In." *Ecumenical Review* 40 (1988): 87–110.

———. "Some Doubts About the Usefulness of the Category 'Evangelical.'" In *The Variety of American Evangelicalism,* ed. Donald W. Dayton and Robert K. Johnston. Knoxville: University of Tennessee Press, 1990.

Dayton, Donald W., and Robert K. Johnston, eds. *The Variety of American Evangelicalism.* Knoxville: University of Tennessee Press, 1990.

DeBerg, Betty A. *Ungodly Women: Gender and the First Wave of American Fundamentalism.* Minneapolis: Fortress Press, 1990.

D'Emilio, John, and Estelle B. Freedman. *Intimate Matters: A History of Sexuality in America.* New York: Harper & Row, 1988.

Demos, John. *A Little Commonwealth: Family Life in Plymouth Colony.* New York: Oxford University Press, 1970.

———. *Past, Present, and Personal: The Family and the Life Course in American History.* New York: Oxford University Press, 1986.

Dwyer-McNulty, Sally. Unpublished field notes, 1993.

Dyson, Clegg. *His Children: A Devotional Guide for the Family.* Boston: Boston Church of Christ, 1984.

Eagleton, Terry. *Ideology: An Introduction.* London: Verso, 1991.

Ebert, Teresa L. *Ludic Feminism and After: Postmodernism, Desire, and Labor in Late Capitalism.* Ann Arbor: University of Michigan Press, 1996.

Echegaray, Hugo. *The Practice of Jesus.* Maryknoll, N.Y.: Orbis, 1984.

Eighmy, John L. *Churches in Cultural Captivity: A History of the Social Attitudes of Southern Baptists.* Knoxville: University of Tennessee Press, 1972.

Emerson, Robert M., Rachel I. Fretz, and Linda L. Shaw. *Writing Ethnographic Fieldnotes.* Chicago: University of Chicago Press, 1995.

Fields, Echo E. 1991. "Understanding Activist Fundamentalism: Capitalist Crisis and the 'Colonization of Lifeworld.'" *Sociological Analysis* 52 (1991): 175–90.

FitzGerald, Frances. "Liberty Baptist." In *Cities on a Hill: A Journey Through Contemporary American Cultures.* New York: Simon & Schuster, 1986.

Flynt, Wayne. "'A Special Feeling of Closeness': Mt. Hebron Baptist Church, Leeds, Alabama." In *American Congregations*, 2 vols., ed. James P. Wind and James W. Lewis. Chicago: University of Chicago Press, 1994.

Franklin, Robert Michael. "The Safest Place on Earth: The Culture of Black Congregations." In *American Congregations*, 2 vols., ed. James P. Wind and James W. Lewis. Chicago: University of Chicago Press, 1994.

Fraser, Nancy. "Rethinking the Public Sphere: A Contribution to the Critique of Actually Existing Democracy." In *Habermas and the Public Sphere*, ed. Craig Calhoun. Cambridge, Mass.: MIT Press, 1992.

Freedman, Samuel G. *Upon This Rock: The Miracles of a Black Church*. New York: HarperCollins, 1993.

Fuchs, Cindy. "The Monkeys Man." *Philadelphia City Paper*, January 5, 1996, 16–18.

Gellner, Ernest. *Conditions of Liberty: Penguin Civil Society and Its Rivals*. New York: Penguin, 1994.

George, Carl F. *Prepare Your Church for the Future*. Grand Rapids, Mich.: Fleming H. Revell, 1992.

Giambarba, Andrew. *Bent on Conquest*. N.p., 1988.

Gilder, George. *Men and Marriage*. Gretna, La.: Pelican, 1995.

Ginsburg, Faye, and Rayna Rapp. "The Politics of Reproduction." *Annual Review of Anthropology* 20 (1991): 311–43.

Gorz, André. *Critique of Economic Reason*. Trans. Gillian Handyside and Chris Turner. London: Verso, 1989.

Graham, Laura. "A Public Sphere in Amazonia? The Depersonalized Collaborative Construction of Discourse in Xavante." *American Ethnologist* 20 (1993): 717–41.

Griffith, Ruth Marie. *God's Daughters*. Berkeley: University of California Press, 1997.

Gutiérrez, Gustavo. *On Job: God-Talk and the Suffering of the Innocent*. Trans. Matthew D. O'Connell. Maryknoll, N.Y.: Orbis, 1987.

Gywn, Douglas. *The Covenant Crucified: Quakers and the Rise of Capitalism*. Wallingford, Pa.: Pendle Hill, 1995.

Habermas, Jürgen. *The Theory of Communicative Action*, 2 vols. Trans. Thomas McCarthy. Boston: Beacon Press, 1985–87.

———. *The Philosophical Discourse of Modernity: Twelve Lectures*. Trans. Frederick Lawrence. Cambridge, Mass.: MIT Press, 1987.

———. *The Structural Transformation of the Public Sphere: An Inquiry into a Category of Bourgeois Society*. Trans. Thomas Burger. Cambridge, Mass.: MIT Press, 1989.

Hacker, Andrew. *Two Nations: Black and White, Separate, Hostile, Unequal*. New York: Scribner, 1992.

Hackett, David. *The Rude Hand of Innovation: Religion and Social Order in Albany, New York, 1652–1836.* New York: Oxford University Press, 1991.

Harding, Susan. "Convicted by the Holy Spirit: The Rhetoric of Fundamental Baptist Conversion." *American Ethnologist* 14 (1987): 167–81.

———. "The World of Born-Again Telescandals." *Michigan Quarterly Review* 27 (1988): 525–40.

———. "If I Should Die Before I Wake: Jerry Falwell's Pro-Life Gospel." In *Uncertain Terms: Renegotiating Gender in American Culture*, ed. Faye Ginsburg and Anna Lowenhaupt Tsing. Boston: Beacon Press, 1990.

Hart, D. G. *Defending the Faith: J. Gresham Machen and the Crisis of Conservative Protestantism in Modern America.* Baltimore: Johns Hopkins University Press, 1994.

———. "The Revolt of the Evangelical Elites: Gender, Equality, and Headship." *Regeneration Quarterly,* Fall 1995, 30–33.

Hart, Stephen. *What Does the Lord Require? How American Christians Think About Economic Justice.* New York: Oxford University Press, 1992.

Hartman, Keith. *Congregations in Conflict: The Battle over Homosexuality.* New Brunswick, N.J.: Rutgers University Press, 1996.

Hayden, Pam. Unpublished field notes, 1992.

Hayes, Kathleen. *Women on the Threshold: Voices of Salvadoran Baptist Women.* Macon, Ga.: Smyth & Helwys, 1996.

Hennelly, Alfred T., ed. *Liberation Theology: A Documentary History.* Maryknoll, N.Y.: Orbis, 1995.

Higginbotham, Evelyn Brooks. *Righteous Discontent: The Women's Movement in the Black Baptist Church, 1880–1920.* Cambridge, Mass.: Harvard University Press, 1993.

Higham, John. "Multiculturalism and Universalism: A History and Critique." *American Quarterly* 45 (1993): 195–219.

Hill, Christopher. *The English Bible and the Seventeenth-Century Revolution.* London: Penguin, 1993.

Hollinger, David A. *Science, Jews, and Secular Culture: Studies in Mid-Twentieth-Century American Intellectual History.* Princeton, N.J.: Princeton University Press, 1996.

Horton, Michael Scott, ed. *Power Religion: The Selling Out of the Evangelical Church?* Chicago: Moody Press, 1992.

Hughes, Richard T. *Reviving the Ancient Faith: The Story of Churches of Christ in America.* Grand Rapids, Mich.: Eerdmans, 1996.

———, ed. *The American Quest for the Primitive Church.* Urbana: University of Illinois Press, 1988.

Hull, Bill. "Is the Church Growth Movement Really Working?" In *Power Religion: The Selling Out of the Evangelical Church?*, ed. Michael Scott Horton. Chicago: Moody Press, 1992.

Hymnal: A Worship Book. Elgin, Ill.: Brethren Press, with Faith and Life Press and Mennonite Publishing House, 1992.

Indiana, Gary. "Press Clips." *Village Voice*, June 19–25, 1996, 16.

Jacoby, Douglas. *The Powerful Delusion.* London: London Church of Christ, 1988.

————. *Shining like Stars.* Lexington, Mass.: Boston Church of Christ, 1990.

Jakobsen, Janet R. "Agency and Alliance in Public Discourse About Sexualities. *Hypatia* 10 (1995): 133–54.

Juhnke, James C. *Vision, Doctrine, War: Mennonite Identity and Organization in America, 1890–1930.* Scottdale, Pa.: Herald Press, 1989.

Karp, Ivan, and Martha B. Kendall. "Reflexivity in Field Work." In *Explaining Human Behavior: Consciousness, Human Action, and Social Structure,* ed. Paul F. Secord. Beverly Hills, Calif.: Sage, 1982.

Kaufman, Gordon D. *In Face of Mystery.* Cambridge, Mass.: Harvard University Press, 1993.

Keane, John. *Public Life and Late Capitalism: Toward a Socialist Theory of Democracy.* Cambridge: Cambridge University Press, 1984.

————. *Civil Society and the State: New European Perspectives.* London: Verso, 1988.

————. *Democracy and Civil Society: On the Predicaments of European Socialism, the Prospects for Democracy, and the Problem of Controlling Social and Political Power.* London: Verso, 1988.

Kellstedt, Lyman, and Mark A. Noll. "Religion, Voting for President, and Party Identification, 1948–1984." *Religion and American Politics: From the Colonial Period to the 1980s,* ed. Mark A. Noll. New York: Oxford University Press, 1990.

Kestenbaum, Herbert, ed. *Regional Almanac 1994.* Philadelphia: Philadelphia Newspapers, 1993.

King, Michael A. "Fractured Dance: Steps and Missteps in Application of Gadamer to a Mennonite Debate on Homosexuality." Ph.D. diss., Temple University, Philadelphia, 1998.

Kintz, Linda. *Between Jesus and the Market: The Emotions That Matter in Right-Wing America.* Durham, N.C.: Duke University Press, 1997.

Kniss, Fred. *Disquiet in the Land.* New Brunswick, N.J.: Rutgers University Press, 1997.

Kosmin, Barry A., and Seymour P. Lachman. "Religious Self-identification." *Yearbook of American and Canadian Churches,* ed. Kenneth B. Bedell. Nashville, Tenn.: Abingdon, 1995.

Kraus, C. Norman. "Evangelicalicalism: A Mennonite Critique." In *Varieties of American Evangelicalism,* ed. Donald W. Dayton and Robert K. Johnston. Knoxville: University of Tennessee Press, 1990.

————, ed. *Evangelicals and Anabaptism.* Scottdale, Pa.: Herald Press, 1979.

Laclau, Ernesto, and Chantal Mouffe. *Hegemony and Socialist Strategy: Towards a Radical Democratic Politics.* London: Verso, 1985.

Laker, Barbara. "Such a Cruel Way to Die." *Philadelphia Daily News*, January 5, 1996, 3.

Lalonde, Marc P. "Power/Knowledge and Liberation." *Journal of the American Academy of Religion* 61 (1993): 81–100.

Lears, T. J. Jackson. "The Concept of Cultural Hegemony: Problems and Possibilities." *American Historical Review* 90 (1985): 567–93.

Leckrone, J. Wesley. "Mennonite Community as an Opposition Movement to Consumer Capitalism." Unpublished manuscript, 1994.

Lederach, Paul M. *A Third Way.* Scottdale, Pa.: Herald Press, 1980.

Le Goff, Jacques. *Your Money or Your Life: Economy and Religion in the Middle Ages.* Cambridge, Mass.: MIT Press, 1988.

Levine, Daniel H. "Popular Groups, Popular Culture, and Popular Religion." *Comparative Studies in Society and History* 32 (1990): 718–64.

Liebow, Elliot. *Tell Them Who I Am: The Lives of Homeless Women.* New York: Penguin, 1993.

Lowe, Donald M. *The Body in Late-Capitalist USA.* Durham, N.C.: Duke University Press, 1995.

Lugones, Maria. 1994. "Purity, Impurity, and Separation." *Signs* 19 (1994): 458–79.

Lukacs, John. *The End of the Twentieth Century.* New York: Ticknor & Fields, 1993.

Lundèn, Rolf. *Business and Religion in the American 1920s.* New York: Greenwood, 1980.

McDannell, Colleen. *The Christian Home in Victorian America, 1840–1900.* Bloomington: Indiana University Press, 1986.

———. *Material Christianity: Religion and Popular Culture in America.* New Haven, Conn.: Yale University Press, 1995.

McGrath, Alister E. "A Better Way: The Priesthood of All Believers." In *Power Religion: The Selling Out of the Evangelical Church?*, ed. Michael Scott Horton. Chicago: Moody Press, 1992.

McKean, Eleana. "Strong to Serve." *UpsideDown*, April 1992, 20–22, 49.

McKean, Kip. "Revolution Through Restoration." *UpsideDown*, April 1992, 5–16.

MacMaster, Richard K. *Land, Piety, Peoplehood: The Establishment of Mennonite Communities in America, 1683–1790.* Scottdale, Pa.: Herald Press, 1985.

Mann, Michael. *The Sources of Social Power.* Cambridge: Cambridge University Press, 1986–1992.

Marsden, George M. "Defining Fundamentalism." *Christian Scholar's Review* 1 (1971): 141–51.

————. *Fundamentalism and American Culture: The Shaping of Twentieth-Century Evangelicalism, 1870–1925.* New York: Oxford University Press, 1980.

————. "Preachers of Paradox: The Religious Right in Historical Perspective." In *Religion and America: Spiritual Life in a Secular Age,* ed. Mary Douglas and Steven Tipton. Boston: Beacon Press, 1982.

————. *Reforming Fundamentalism: Fuller Seminary and the New Evangelicalism.* Grand Rapids, Mich.: Eerdmans, 1987.

Marty, Martin E. "Public and Private: Congregation as Meeting Place." In *American Congregations,* 2 vols., ed. James P. Wind and James W. Lewis. Chicago: University of Chicago Press, 1994.

Marty, Martin E., and Scott R. Appleby, eds. *Fundamentalisms Observed.* Fundamentalism Project 1. Chicago: University of Chicago Press, 1991.

Matthew, Miles B., and Michael A. Huberman. *Qualitative Data Ananlysis.* Beverly Hills, Calif.: Sage, 1984.

Matthiessen, Peter. *At Play in the Fields of the Lord.* New York: Random House, 1965.

May, Elaine Tyler. *Homeward Bound: American Families in the Cold War Era.* New York: Basic Books, 1988.

Melton, J. Gordon. *National Directory of Churches, Synagogues, and Other Houses of Worship.* Detroit: Gale Research, 1994.

Miller, Donald E. *Reinventing American Protestantism: Christianity in the New Millennium.* Berkeley: University of California Press, 1997.

Miller, Keith Graber. *Wise as Serpents, Innocent as Doves: American Mennonites Engage Washington.* Knoxville: University of Tennessee Press, 1996.

Moore, R. Laurence. *Selling God: American Religion in the Marketplace of Culture.* New York: Oxford University Press, 1994.

Moulton, Phillips S., ed. *The Journal and Major Essays of John Woolman.* Richmond, Ind.: Friends United Press, 1989.

Mount, Ferdinand. *The Subversive Family: An Alternative History of Love and Marriage.* New York: Free Press, 1992.

Myers, Ched. *Binding the Strong Man: A Political Reading of Mark's Story of Jesus.* Maryknoll, N.Y.: Orbis, 1988.

Nash, Gary B., and Julie Roy Jeffrey, eds. *The American People: Creating a Nation and a Society.* New York: Longman, 1998.

Noll, Mark A., Nathan O. Hatch, and George M. Marsden. *The Search for Christian America,* rev. ed. Colorado Springs, Col.: Helmers & Howard, 1989.

O'Connor, Flannery. *Three by Flannery O'Connor.* New York: Signet, 1962.

O'Hara, Daniel T. "Class." In *Critical Terms for Literary Studies,* 2nd ed., ed. Frank Lentricchia and Thomas McLaughlin. Chicago: University of Chicago Press, 1995.

Orsi, Robert Anthony. *The Madonna of 115th Street: Faith and Community in Italian Harlem, 1880–1950*. New Haven, Conn.: Yale University Press, 1985.

Parker, Janet L. 1996. "Religious, 'Right,' and Heterosexist." *Conscience*, Spring 1996, 3–14.

Patton, Cindy. *Sex and Germs: The Politics of AIDS*. Boston: South End Press, 1985.

Peshkin, Alan. *God's Choice: The Total World of a Fundamentalist Christian School*. Chicago: University of Chicago Press, 1986.

Piercy, Marge. 1996. "The Fundamental Truth." *Tikkun*, January/February 1996, inside front cover.

Piper, John, and Wayne Grundem, eds. *Recovering Biblical Manhood and Womanhood*. Wheaton, Ill.: Crossway, 1991.

Poggi, Gianfranco. *The Development of the Modern State: A Sociological Introduction*. Stanford, Calif.: Stanford University Press, 1978.

———. *The State: Its Nature, Development and Prospects*. Stanford, Calif.: Stanford University Press, 1990.

Postman, Neil. *Amusing Ourselves to Death: Public Discourse in the Age of Show Business*. New York: Penguin, 1985.

Pratt, Minnie Bruce. *Rebellion*. Ithaca, N.Y.: Firebrand Books, 1991.

Primer, Ben. *Protestants and American Business Methods*. Ann Arbor, Mich.: UMI Research Press, 1979.

Redekop, Calvin. *Mennonite Society*. Baltimore: Johns Hopkins University Press, 1989.

Ribuffo, Leo P. *The Old Christian Right: The Protestant Far Right from the Great Depression to the Cold War*. Philadelphia: Temple University Press, 1983.

———. "God and Contemporary Politics." *Journal of American History* 79 (1993): 1515–33.

Rich, Adrienne. "Compulsory Heterosexuality and Lesbian Experience." In *Blood, Bread, and Poetry*. New York: Norton, 1986.

Richardson, Alan, and John Bowden, eds. *The Westminster Dictionary of Christian Theology*. Philadelphia: Westminster Press, 1983.

Roozen, David A., William McKinnery, and Jackson W. Carroll. *Varieties of Religious Presence: Mission in Public Life*. New York: Pilgrim Press, 1984.

Rose, Gillian. *Love's Work: A Reckoning with Life*. New York: Schocken, 1995.

Rose, Susan D. *Keeping Them Out of the Hands of Satan: Evangelical Schooling in America*. New York: Routledge, 1988.

Saskia, Sassen. "Economic Restructuring and the American City." *Annual Review of Sociology* 16 (1990): 465–90.

Schiller, Herbert I. *Culture, Inc.: The Corporate Takeover of Public Expression*. New York: Oxford University Press, 1989.

Schlabach, Theron F. *Peace, Faith, Nation: Mennonites and Amish in Nineteenth-Century America*. Scottdale, Pa.: Herald Press, 1985.

Schmidt, Leigh Eric. *Consumer Rites: The Buying and Selling of American Holidays*. Princeton, N.J.: Princeton University Press, 1995.

Schneider, David M. *American Kinship: A Cultural Account*, 2nd ed. Chicago: University of Chicago Press, 1980.

Schor, Juliet. *The Overworked American: The Unexpected Decline in Leisure*. New York: Basic Books, 1991

Schutz, Alfred, and Thomas Luckmann. *The Structures of the Life-World*. Trans. Richard M. Zaner and H. Tristram Englehart, Jr. Evanston, Ill.: Northwestern University Press, 1973.

Schwartz, Regina M. *The Curse of Cain: The Violent Legacy of Monotheism*. Chicago: University of Chicago Press, 1997.

Scott, James C. 1990. *Domination and the Arts of Resistance*. New Haven, Conn.: Yale University Press, 1990.

Sinha, Surajit. "Religion in an Affluent Society." *Current Anthropology* 7 (1966): 189–95.

Smith, Joan, and Immanuel Wallerstein, eds. *Creating and Transforming Households: The Constraints of the World Economy*. Cambridge: Cambridge University Press, 1992.

Smith, Timothy L. 1986. "The Evangelical Kaleidoscope and the Call to Christian Unity." *Christian Scholar's Review* 15 (1986): 125–40.

Stacey, Judith. *Brave New Families: Stories of Domestic Upheaval in Late Twentieth Century America*. New York: Basic Books, 1990.

———. "Scents, Scholars, and Stigma: The Revisionist Campaign for Family Values." *Social Text* 40 (1994): 51–76.

Steedman, Carolyn Kay. *Landscape for a Good Woman: The Story of Two Lives*. New Brunswick, N.J.: Rutgers University Press, 1994.

Stein, Stephen J. *The Shaker Exerience in America*. New Haven, Conn.: Yale University Press, 1992.

Stohler, Steve G. "The Evangelical Subculture." *Voice*, May–June 1992, 8.

[Stuart], Thomas S. "Fundamentalism, American Capitalism, and Culture." Unpublished manuscript, 1994.

Sweeney, Douglas A. "The Essential Evangelicalism Dialectic: The Historiography of the Early Neo-Evangelical Movement and the Observer-Participant Dilemma." *Church History* 60 (1991): 70–84.

Sweet, Leonard I. 1988. "Wise as Serpents, Innocent as Doves: The New Evangelical Historiography." *Journal of the American Academy of Religion* 56 (1988): 397–416.

Taves, Ann. *The Household of Faith: Roman Catholic Devotions in Mid-Nineteenth-Century America*. Notre Dame, Ind.: Notre Dame University Press, 1986.

Thomas, George M. *Revivalism and Cultural Change: Christianity, Nation Building, and the Market in the Nineteenth-Century United States*. Chicago: University of Chicago Press, 1989.

Thomas, Jim. *Doing Critical Ethnography*. Newbury Park, Calif.: Sage, 1993.

Tilly, Charles. "Retrieving European Lives." In *Reliving the Past: The Worlds of Social History*, ed. Olivier Zunz. Chapel Hill: University of North Carolina Press, 1985.

————. *Coercion, Capital, and European States, AD 990–1990*. Cambridge, Mass.: Blackwell, 1990.

Titon, Jeff Todd. *Powerhouse for God: Sacred Speech, Chant, and Song in an Appalachian Baptist Church*. Austin: University of Texas Press, 1988.

Toews, Paul. *Mennonites in American Society, 1930–1970*. Scottdale, Pa.: Herald Press, 1996.

Tomaskovic-Devey, Donald. "The Protestant Ethic, the Christian Right and the Spirit of Recapitalization." In *The Political Role of Religion in the United States*. Boulder, Col.: Westview Press, 1986.

Tweed, Thomas A., ed. *Retelling U.S. Religious History*. Berkeley: University of California Press, 1997.

Van Maanen, John. *Tales of the Field: On Writing Ethnography*. Chicago: University of Chicago Press, 1988.

Veer, Peter van der, ed. *Conversion to Modernities: The Globalization of Christianity*. New York: Routledge, 1996.

Veyne, Paul. *Writing History*. Middletown, Conn.: Wesleyan University Press, 1971.

Visweswaran, Kamala. *Fictions of Feminist Ethnography*. Minneapolis: University of Minnesota Press, 1994.

Wacker, Grant. "Searching for Norman Rockwell: Popular Evangelicalism in Contemporary America." In *The Evangelical Tradition in America*, ed. Leonard I. Sweet. Macon, Ga.: Mercer University Press, 1984.

————. "Uneasy in Zion: Evangelicals in Postmodern Society." In *Evangelicalism and Modern America*, ed. George M. Marsden. Grand Rapids, Mich.: Eerdmans, 1984.

————. *Augustus H. Strong and the Dilemma of Historical Consciousness*. Macon, Ga.: Mercer University Press, 1985.

————. "The Holy Spirit and the Spirit of the Age in American Protestantism, 1880–1910." *Journal of American History* 72 (1985): 45–62.

Wagner, Melinda Bollar. *God's Schools: Choice and Compromise in American Society*. New Brunswick, N.J.: Rutgers University Press, 1990.

Wallerstein, Immanuel. "World Systems Analysis." In *Social Theory Today*, ed. Anthony Giddens and Jonathan H. Turner. Stanford, Calif.: Stanford University Press, 1987.

————. *Unthinking Social Science: The Limits of Nineteenth-Century Paradigms*. Cambridge: Polity Press, 1991.

Warner, Michael, ed. *Fear of a Queer Planet: Queer Politics and Social Theory*. Minneapolis: University of Minnesota Press, 1993.

Warner, R. Stephen. *New Wine in Old Wineskins: Evangelicals and Liberals in a Small-Town Church*. Berkeley: University of California Press, 1988.

———. "Work in Progress Toward a New Paradigm for the Sociological Study of Religion in the United States." *American Journal of Sociology* 98 (1993): 1044–93.

Watt, David Harrington. "Religion and the Nation: 1960 to the Present." In *Church and State in America: A Bibliographic Guide*, ed. John F. Wilson. Westport, Conn.: Greenwood Press, 1987.

———. "Evangelicalism, the Market, and the State in Nineteenth-Century America." *Evangelical Studies Bulletin* 8 (1991): 1–3.

———. *A Transforming Faith: Explorations of Twentieth-Century American Evangelicalism*. New Brunswick, N.J.: Rutgers University Press, 1991.

———. Unpublished fieldnotes, 1991–94.

Waugh, Earle H. 1997. "Fundamentalism: Harbinger of Academic Revisionism?" *Journal of the American Academy of Religion* 65 (1997): 161–68.

Wax, Rosalie H. *Doing Fieldwork: Warnings and Advice*. Chicago: University of Chicago Press, 1971.

Weber, Paul J., and W. Landis Jones. *U.S. Religious Interest Groups*. Westport, Conn.: Greenwood Press, 1994.

Weber, Timothy P. *Living in the Shadow of the Second Coming: American Premillennialism, 1875–1982*. Chicago: University of Chicago Press, 1987.

Welch, Sharon D. *Communities of Resistance and Solidarity: A Feminist Theology of Liberation*. Maryknoll, N.Y.: Orbis, 1985.

Werner, Oswald, and Mark G. Schoepfle. *Systematic Fieldwork*. Beverly Hills, Calif.: Sage, 1987.

White, Stephen K. *The Recent Work of Jürgen Habermas: Reason, Justice, and Modernity*. New York: Cambridge University Press, 1988.

———. *Political Theory and Postmodernism*. New York: Cambridge University Press, 1991.

Wilcox, Clyde. "Premillennialists at the Millennium." *Sociology of Religion* 55 (1994): 243–62.

Williams, Raymond. "Base and Superstructure in Marxist Cultural Theory." In *Problems in Materialism and Culture: Selected Essays*. London: Verso, 1980.

Wind, James P., and James W. Lewis, eds. *American Congregations*, 2 vols. Chicago: University of Chicago Press, 1994.

Wittig, Monique. *The Straight Mind and Other Essays*. Boston: Beacon Press, 1992.

Wolcott, Harry F. *The Art of Fieldwork*. Walnut Creek, Calif.: AltaMira Press, 1995.

Wolfe, Eric R. *Europe and the People Without History*. Berkeley: University of California Press, 1990.

Wuthnow, Robert. *The Restructuring of American Religion*. Princeton, N.J.: Princeton University Press, 1988.

————. *God and Mammon in America*. New York: Free Press, 1994.

Yearly Meeting of the Religious Society of Friends in Britain. *Quaker Faith and Practice*. Warwick, England: Warwick Printing, 1995.

Zuckerman, Michael. "Holy Wars, Civil Wars." *Prospects: An Annual of American Cultural Studies* 16 (1991): 205–40.

Zweig, Michael, ed. *Religion and Economic Justice*. Philadelphia: Temple University Press, 1991.

INDEX

abortion, 12
Accelerated Christian Education, 39,
  49
African Americans, 17–18, 92, 142n.22
Alabama, 29, 30
American flag, 32, 46, 71, 72, 109
Amherst, Douglas, 95
Arato, Andrew, 25
asymmetrical power, 23–29, 115, 133n.2

Balmer, Randall, 25
Baptists, 30, 92
Bateson, Susan, 52
beast (Revelation to John), 73
beauty, 112
Bent on Conquest (Giambarba), 97–98
Bevilacqua, Cardinal Anthony J., 12
Bible, 23–24, 64–66, 80, 81, 89, 103–4,
  117
Bible-carrying Christian churches, 4–5
  asymmetrical power, 24–29, 115
  and big government, 26, 27–28
  and corporations, 25–26, 27, 117–18
  counternarrative on, 28–29
  as educational organizations, 27
  1957 to 1973, 29–33
  and patriotism, 26
  and social power, 26
  and submission to authority, 27
  See also specific churches
big government, 26, 27–28, 37–38
Black Clergy of Philadelphia, 12, 14
blacks. *See* African Americans

blackwashing, 14
Blackwell, Cory, 96
"Blest Be the Tie That Binds," 32–33
Bob Jones University, 36
Boswell, John, 24
Bright, Bill, 6
bureaucracy, 26
Burke, Gloria, 52
Bush, George, 17
business, 18, 47–48, 49–50
"Business of Belief, The" (Comens),
  50

Calvert, Terry, 101–5, 107
Calvin, John, 25
capitalism, 49–50, 134n.14
Center City (Philadelphia, Pa.), 15,
  16
ceremonies and rituals, 74, 76
chief executive officers (CEOs),
  18
children, 80
Christian congregations, 3–5
Civil Society and Political Theory
  (Cohen and Arato), 25
Clinton, Bill, 17
Cohen, Jean, 25
Comens, Bruce, 50, 68–69, 99
commerce, 78–79
conscientious objectors, 62
conservative Protestants, 4
consumer goods, 105–9
corporations, 25–26, 27, 50, 116–18